When the sea turned to beer:

a hoard of humour, history & Heathenry.

by

Pete Jennings

GRUFF BOOKS

PETE JENNINGS
12 CARLTON CLOSE, GREAT YELDHAM, HALSTEAD, ESSEX
CO9 4QJ
TEL 01787 238257 / 07778 366469
www.gippeswic.org
gippeswic@btinternet.com

Other Books & eBooks by Pete Jennings

Pathworking (with Pete Sawyer) – Capall Bann (1993)
Northern Tradition Information Pack – Pagan Federation (1996)
Supernatural Ipswich – Gruff (1997)
Pagan Paths – Rider (2002)
The Northern Tradition – Capall Bann (2003)
Mysterious Ipswich – Gruff (2003)
Old Glory & the Cutty Wren – Gruff (2003)
Pagan Humour – Gruff (2005)
The Gothi & the Rune Stave – Gruff (2005)
Haunted Suffolk – Tempus (2006)
Tales & Tours – Gruff (2006)
Haunted Ipswich – Tempus/ History Press (2010)
Penda: Heathen King of Mercia and his Anglo-Saxon World. – Gruff (2013)
The Wild Hunt & its followers – Gruff (2013)
Blacksmith Gods, Myths, Magicians & Folklore – Moon Books- Pagan Portals (2014)
Heathen Information Pack (with others) – Pagan Federation (2014)
Confidently Confused – Gruff (2014)
Adventures in Ælphame – Gruff (2015)
Valkyries, selectors of heroes: their roles within Viking & Anglo-Saxon heathen beliefs. - Gruff (2016)
A Cacophony of Corvids: the mythology, facts, behaviour and folklore of ravens, crows, magpies and their relatives. - Gruff (2017)
Heathen Paths (2nd expanded & revised edition): Viking and Anglo-Saxon Pagan Beliefs – Gruff (2018)
The Bounds of Ælphame – Gruff (2019)
The Woodwose in Suffolk & beyond. – Gruff (2019)
Pathworking & Creative Visualisation – Gruff (2019)
Viking Warrior Cults – Gruff (2019)

Pete Jennings has also contributed to:

Modern Pagans: an investigation of contemporary Pagan practices. (Eds. V Vale & J. Sulak.) San Francisco: RE/Search (2001)
The Museum of Witchcraft: A Magical History – (Ed. Kerriann Godwin) Boscastle: Occult Art Co. (2011)

Heathen Information Pack – UK: Pagan Federation (2014)
The Call of the God: an anthology exploring the divine masculine within modern Paganism (Ed. Frances Billinghurst) Australia: TDM (2015)
Pagan Planet: Being, Believing & Belonging in the 21st Century. Ed. Nimue Brown. UK: Moon Books (2016)

Recordings

Awake (with WYSIWYG) – Homebrew (1987)
Chocks Away (with WYSIWYG) Athos (1988)
No Kidding (with Pyramid of Goats) – Gruff (1990)
Spooky Suffolk (with Ed Nicholls) Gruff (2003)
Old Glory & the Cutty Wren CD – Gruff (2003)

Films that Pete has featured in

Suffolk Ghosts – Directed by Richard Felix. Past in Pictures, 2005
Wild Hunt – Directed by Will Wright. Film Tribe, 2006
In search of Beowulf with Michael Wood BBC4, 2009
Born of Hope – Directed by Kate Maddison – Actors at Work 2009
The Last Journey – Directed by Carl Stickley, 2018

Find details of how to obtain these books and an up to date diary of lectures and appearances by Pete Jennings at www.gippeswic.org
Some books are available as hard copy and electronic digital versions via
www.amazon.co.uk/Pete-Jennings/e/B0034OPQP8

Pete regularly writes shorter magazine articles and reviews, especially for *Widowinde, Witchcraft & Wicca, Pagan Dawn* and *Pentacle.* He was also the editor of the *Gippeswic* magazine.

You can also follow Pete Jennings & *Ealdfaeder Anglo Saxons* on Facebook.
For appearances of Pete with his *Ealdfaeder Anglo Saxons* re-enactor friends, plus lots of information on Anglo Saxon topics go to www.ealdfaeder.org

About the Author

Pete Jennings was born in Ipswich, Suffolk in 1953. He has had careers as a telephone engineer, sales manager and has recently retired as a registered social worker. He is also a registered psychotherapist and now lives on the Essex / Suffolk border. Some people are held up as shining examples to others; Pete prefers to be a dreadful warning.

Outside of his inner working life, he has sung with rock and folk bands, been a disco deejay and radio presenter, Anglo Saxon & Viking re-enactor, actor, artist, ghost tour guide, storyteller & Pagan activist. He has had over twenty books published and regularly lectures in the UK and abroad.

He has a low boredom threshold, likes dogs, 70s prog rock, books, folk traditions, weird humour, real ale and his wife Sue, but not necessarily in that order. One day he hopes to be recognised for his pioneering research on the Speed of Dark.

Foreword

Welcome to a collection of short stories, articles, poems and other odd (distinctly odd in some places) bits of writing from me over the last few decades. They are divided between the serious and humorous, but you may have to make your mind up about which category they fall within. Some have been published before in some shape or form but are now out of print. Other material was written especially for this compilation or dug out of old files and re-edited. There is no theme or link between the pieces, other than they have come from a head which has been set on fire twice, which may explain a lot. I make no apology to anyone I offend in this writing, except to those whom I have missed out.

Pete Jennings – 2020

Index

The archaeologist

(Originating from a challenge to write a story in 300 words)

"Damn the politicians' funding cuts!" muttered Jim to himself. He cleared away soil in his mud-stained high visibility archaeologist's jacket. The romance of the job had long left him, buried beneath layers as deep as the Cambrian Period. He was on a grassy roundabout, so nobody peered into his excavation over the flimsy barrier. Passing motorists probably took him for a gas engineer and choked him with their exhaust fumes. He wearily climbed the ladder to haul soil up in a bucket, which he flung onto a growing spoil heap.

Although he found no artefacts or even interestingly stained subsoil, Jim continued his lonely quest all day. He scowled to himself about ground radar and drone cameras. Forget teams of students digging trenches. University fees and a dismal career path had given way to mechanical mini diggers. Jim felt as obsolete as the Saxon wrist clasp that had been his first exciting find so many years ago.

Satellite systems had mainly overtaken his skill at interpreting old maps. He snorted to himself in bitter derision as he worked methodically. He'd dug down to six feet now, and then burrowed sideways a few yards to where he encountered some carved stones, with flakes of mediaeval plaster.

Later, relaxing on a sunbed in the Caribbean with a refreshing drink to his lips, Jim reflected that his talents hadn't altogether been wasted. It was almost a week before the bank had discovered the hole in the floor at the back of their vault. It dropped down through the ceiling of the monastery cellar below. They really should have checked into the quaint plan of the ruined old monastery that their edifice was constructed above, despite local objections. Jim had kept it as a souvenir along with the money.

Ascending Yggdrasill

The mysterious rhythm of the runes, the
eloquence of the saga stories and the awful
finality of oath sworn oratory: let me lead you
into the corner of the Web of Wyrd that is forever
Heathen. Few politically correct vegetarian
pacifists are drawn to this bad boy of the Pagan
paths: yet the joy it brings to its' Asatru
adherents is palpable, passionate and poetic.

Heathen is a word very much like Pagan in
meaning. In essence, both indicate people living
in the heath or country, with the subtle difference
that while Pagan is derived from Latin, Heathen
is born out of the Germanic languages of
Northern Europe, from where its majestic
mythology and beliefs found their roots before
blossoming in Gt. Britain, Ireland, Scandinavia,
Iceland, Greenland and even North America and
Russia. It is a collection of many similar folk
beliefs with notable regional variations,
pronunciations and flavours.

There are over a hundred deities known by both
Norse and Anglo-Saxon names, from the well-
known Odin (Woden), Thor (Thunor), Tyr (Tiw)
Frigga and Balder to the lesser-known Hoenir,
Mimir and Saga, all of the Aesir family. If you are
a witch and address the Lord and Lady within
your rites, have you ever thought how their
names are the translation of the major Vanir god
& goddess Frey & Freyja? There are also the

Disir, female ancestor spirits that are reverenced for their presence and guidance. Do not forget that the first recorded witch execution in England (by drowning) was in the Anglo-Saxon period at Peterborough in 948 for a woman that used an effigy to ill wish a man called Ælfsige.

Witchcraft is not an art much associated with Heathens, yet a few of us do attempt to work magic, and so by that broad definition, I count myself one, in defiance of some of my comrades. There are, of course, powerful witches such as Groa who aid the gods at their request within the rich and complex mythology. Light and Dark Elves, Dwarves, Trolls and Etin Thurz Giants also have their places within the nine realms of our sacred world tree, Yggdrasill, positioned above the primal abyss/ void Ginnugagap. There is more than one form of Northern Tradition magic though: The Volva seeress and male Seidreman use the intuitive Seidr magic taught by the Vanir Goddess Freyja to the Aesir Allfather Odin. It includes leechcraft, the use of herbs and can draw on written Anglo-Saxon examples such as the Nine Herbs Charm and Erce Erce. Other practices include trance divination from a high seat and singing chants. The Aesir have their Galdr magic, a more ceremonial form involving formal rituals and celebrations practised by the Gothi & Gytha, the priest and priestess. Yet all borrow from each other: the two sources are not incompatible. The best-known magic of all to outsiders to our tradition are the runes, an alphabet script for reading and writing (with many regional variants), powerful chants and sigils, yet also a divinatory tool.

The wonderful stories have powerful hidden meanings and alliteration. They are also instructive and inspirational. Where would Tolkien, Wagner and Jung have been without their intricate motifs? The heroic Anglo-Saxon tale of Beowulf rubs shoulders with the Icelandic saga of Egil and the Germanic Wayland Smithy. We are very fortunate that many Old English and Old Norse literature details rituals and magical practices (even if it is Christians explicitly forbidding what was done!) Although we do not have a complete picture, we probably have a better documented idea of Heathen practices then than almost any other modern Pagan path with the probable exception of the Egyptians. Whether then one chooses to copy them slavishly or use them as a basis for creating more modern beliefs and ceremonies more suitable to the current context is up to the individual. Although we do not have a specific holy book, the Icelandic Havamal ('sayings of the High One') is an influential text on the ways that we try to conduct ourselves, with an emphasis on self-reliance, maintaining loyalty and securing a good reputation.

Central to this is a complex, almost untranslatable word called 'Troth. This encompasses these qualities and many more, such as taking personal responsibility for our actions. It ranges from environmentalism to how we respond to attacks upon us and our kith and kin. We have no equivalent to the Wiccan Rede of "An it harm none." Although most of us do not seek conflict, most of us regard physically protecting homes and families as a specific religious duty, so do not rely upon us to stand meekly by for a burglar muttering about his karma!

It is at this point where some readers may pause and say, "but weren't the Saxons and Vikings a lot of drunken pillaging warrior types?" Fair comment, but in that those elite warrior classes were very similar to those in the cuddly Celtic worlds. Take a look at the artwork of these peoples, and you very soon realise that they lived in anything but a 'Dark Age.' A man could not be recognised as a proper leader unless he could compose poetry to fiendish metres and clever alliteration, as well as excel at board games and riddles. The jewellery of the men and women is some of the most exquisite ever known, and they gave England the basis of its law codes and compensation structures, much of our language and even place names and the days of the week: Tiwsday, Wodensday, Thunorsday, Friggaday.

Heathenism (or to give its other names Odinism, Northern tradition and Asatru) has suffered in the past from far right-wing racist and homophobic extremists trying to tap into its powerful iconography for their twisted ends. It is a problem that most religions suffer from, and the Neo-Nazi is no more a typical Heathen than the Klu Klux Klan are typical Christians. The majority of Heathens are very wary of extremists of any form and distance themselves from them.

The Heathen methodology is radically different from the more familiar ones used by modern witches: the Vé ritual space is rectangular, not round. Blessings are made with the sign of a Thor's hammer (Mjollnir) rather than a pentagram, and meat and mead are more popular as the constituents for the ritual feast than cakes and ale. Few wear any special clothing, but some may wear arm rings and Thorshammer or Valknut pendants or tattoos. There are only two elements: fire and ice, although one may perceive that fire contains air and ice has to rest on earth as well as be made from water. The polarity of the sun is female (warm and inviting), and the moon male (cold and hard) are in contrast to the more usual 'hot & fiery male' and 'dark and mysterious female.' They are all stereotypes, of course, and I guess we all know people who act in the reverse roles to those specified by their gender attributes. In any case, our writings inform us that the Gods and Goddesses are equal and echoing that there is no established hierarchical dominance within ritual for either gender. It has been said though that there are more male Heathens than female, although the balance has swung in the last few years to reduce the disparity in numbers.

Neither do Heathens have an eightfold wheel of the year. Winterfinding, Summerfinding and Mothers Night are our only traditional festivals, but being mainly gregarious we add other 'blots' (a ritual word derived from blood sacrifice) as we wish. Like our ancestors, those rites may be in an indoor temple or outside within natural settings. The Anglo-Saxon word hearg refers to an outside altar and gives us place names with 'Harrow' in them. At those celebrations, we are likely to welcome the deities, wights and ancestors, and drink ritual toasts to them, most often from a shared drinking horn of mead. This is known as a sumbel. There may also be oaths taken, sworn on an arm ring. Weapons are historically not allowed within the sacred space. Oaths are very important within this spiritual path, and keeping them enhances individual, and group reputation and luck called hamingja. It is created within a set of universal laws sometimes referred to as orlög in Old Norse or Wyrd in Old English.

Belief will inevitably be individual to each Heathen, even if they belong to a collective Hearth group, and the views I have expressed here are purely personal and do not necessarily represent the ideas of others with which I am associated. That is how it should be, with each Heathen finding their interpretation of the material they study, and their practical experiences and meditations. I leave you with a Heathen blessing, common in both Old English and Old Norse, and meaning 'be hale and hearty.'

Waes Hael!

Traditional East Anglian Weather Almanac

Old weather sayings contain a lot of truth, as can be seen in the explanations here:

1.   Frost on hawthorn – David Jason will rip his trousers.
2.   If you see a cowslip – call a vet.
3.   Red sky at night – someone bought a weekend cottage in Southwold.
4.   When the wind blows from the East, Baked beans have been a feast.
5.   When seaweed is wet – it's raining.
6.   When at first you find the Sun, ignore it and buy a proper newspaper.
7.   It only rains once a year in Wisbech – for a whole 11 months.
8.   If you can't see Ely Cathedral from Stuntney, it's foggy. If you can see it, that'll
        be foggy soon.
9.   The reason why there are April showers is we can't afford heating bills for the   rest of the year.
10.   (Shakespeare, The Tempest) "When milk comes frozen home in pail" –   You've bought the giant size McFlurry.
11.   If you laid all the weathermen head to toes in a straight line, they still wouldn't   point in the same direction.
12.   If you hear a Tornado, the RAF are sure to appear.
13.   When cows lie down in the meadow, it's a sure sign they're knackered.

14. Never cast a clout until May is out: if you see that girl May give her a thump for me.

15. The March winds will blow,
And we shall have snow
The country will stop
And broadband goes slow.

16. When rooks go to sleep early, you've just lost at chess.

17. When the canary flies northwards, Ipswich Town have beaten Norwich again.

18. If you hear the first cuckoo, it means that someone has bought an annoying clock.

19. If it rains on St Swithin's Day, it will rain for 40 days more. Or less.

20. John McEnroe is useless at forecasting weather for Wimbledon. When he sees clouds, all he ever says is 'it can't be Sirius.'

Weaving Magic

Written for the COA 'Witchcraft & Wicca' magazine.

We talk about weaving magic in a general way, but have you ever considered how textiles have been historically used in magic? Some of the techniques are still applicable today, even if the required results may be more ethical.

Consider the case of the Viking Sigurd, who was due to face a vastly superior army in battle with his men: his mother wove him a Raven Banner. (The raven has long been associated with battlefields as carrion.) The banner enabled him to face and defeat armies of up to seven times the size of his own. However, all magic has its' price, and the cost of this magic was that the bearer of the banner would die in the battle. Not a popular job with prospects then!

Then there is another Viking in that same Orkneyingsaga called Harold Smooth Tongue. He is hoping to assume control as the new Earl of Orkney, but his brother Paul is also trying to do the same. He wakes up one morning and walks through to the front of the house, where his Mother and Auntie Frakok are just finishing making a fancy shirt with gold thread decoration. "Ah! Just the thing" he says, going to put the shirt on. "No, don't, it is for your brother Paul. We will find you another shirt" the women plead.

"Huh, don't make shirts for him, it is me that is going to be the new Earl of Orkney" he replied, seizing the shirt and putting it on. A few minutes later, Harold Smooth Tongue was writhing in agony on the ground and died. The shirt had been poisoned and spells woven into it to kill his brother, but the plan had backfired.

Consequently, his brother Paul became the Earl and was faced with judging what to do with his auntie and mother. They had tried to kill him, but their attempt had led to him being successful, so rather than having them executed, he had them exiled. Looking at this it could be seen as negative or positive magic I guess, depending on whose side you were on, but it wouldn't pass the test for many magicians' codes of ethics nowadays.

Negative it may be, but it shows us the principle of using textiles as a carrier of magic, which can be adapted to modern magical practices. On a moral point, would they have been better to have woven a shirt of 'success' magic for their favoured relative? Ethically it would still be harming his rival, albeit as a side effect. We must always look to how our actions affect other people and events as the reverberations spread across the Web of the Wyrd. Of course, that Web of the Wyrd itself is said to be woven by the Three Norns of Norse mythology: Urd, Verdandi & Skuld. (Fate, Being and Necessity respectively.) One tale tells of them using human entrails as the warp and weft, skulls as loom weights and bones as weaving battens. Even the Gods are fearful of their powers as they decide the ultimate fate of each person.

OK, so there we have a couple of bloodthirsty examples from my Heathen tradition. Still, I am sure you can find many other gentler examples of spinning, weaving and stitching cloth within other mythologies and folk tales such as Rumpelstiltskin. Some goddesses even have a distaff (for spinning wool into a thread) as their symbol, showing the importance of this activity. The Germanic Frau Holle is one, but there are other spinning and weaving goddesses around the world such as the Greek Arachne, Finnish Paivatar and Norse Frigga. Some of the mythology and folktales involving weaving inevitably include an element of being connected to spiders and their webs.

How to adapt these sources for modern magical practice is a wide-open subject. You could, for example, embroider protective sigils such as a pentagram, triskele, runes or ogham script onto clothing or the bag in which you keep a precious object. The container may physically protect the crystal, jewellery or wand, but the symbols on it could give it magical protection. Why not incorporate magic into your robes, altar cloth or banners? If you are stitching a hem, why not meditate on each stitch and repeat a word or phrase to build up the magic. E.g. 'protection' or 'luck.'

Funnily enough, a popular way of incorporating symbolism within clothing is often not considered: printed t-shirts. I, for example, sometimes wear one with the protective aegilshamr (helm of awe) Icelandic bindrune pattern printed on the chest. If you cannot obtain a T-shirt with the symbology you want, how much better would it be to use fabric paints to put your design onto a plain t-shirt? Or you could embroider a t-shirt, blouse, sweatshirt etc. or stitch fabric shapes onto it. Coloured ribbon is useful for creating narrow symbols such as runes, ogham or a pentagram. One can even purchase 'print it yourself' t-shirt transfer kits which can take an image from a computer and turn it into a reversed image transfer, necessary for it to appear the right way around eventually.

Plaiting and knotting a cord to tie around a robe is another way of incorporating personal magic into your robes and is used within some witch traditions. You can use different colours of cord to braid together, with each colour signifying a particular quality, such as 'peace' 'concentration' 'ethical.' Each time you use it, you will be reminded of the magic, and the idea of having a meditation or prayer connected with each item of ritual clothing isn't restricted to Paganism. In essence, it is used for example by Roman Catholic priests for their ceremonial vestments.

Make sure that the colour used resonates with your own beliefs and correspondences, rather than following someone else's example just because 'it says so in a book.' Many people use green to signify the power of nature, but an old friend of mine uses red: he has always regarded the phrase 'nature red in tooth and claw' as an essential truth within his own beliefs, so it is appropriate that he uses a colour that reflects that rather than slavishly follow everyone else. We are Pagans and should think for ourselves!

The Idiot Tree

The Idiot Tree *(Arborus Ignoramus)* grows successfully in almost any type of soil or weather conditions and can thus be found in every continent of the world. It is a hardy perennial which fruits throughout the year. In the village subspecies, it may only produce a single fruit, known as the village idiot. Still, it fruits abundantly in larger metropolitan areas, mainly due to a nutrient-rich diet comprised of fast food, media frenzy and social fashions.

There have been allegations that as a useless and invasive weed it should be controlled or eradicated, but the virulent spread of the species has now made this logistically impossible. It seems immune to Darwinism (survival of the fittest) methods and is now threatening to eliminate all other species by spreading into their natural habitat.

The only known effective predator on it seems to be *Grumpus Agus Personus*, but tight governmental controls over biodiversity have limited their effect. Indeed, Westminster appears to be the most fertile environment for this pernicious species. There is a suspicion that the government has allowed a genetically modified super-resistant subspecies to be developed under the secretive EM-PEE Programme.

I would appreciate receiving any further research data on this subject.

Saint Chads Well, Norfolk.

Published initially in Wiðowinde, the Journal of The English Companions (Ða Engliscan Gesiðas)

According to Bede and his first-hand sources at Lastingham, Saint Chad (Ceadda) was one of four brothers who studied the Celtic form of Christianity at Lindisfarne under St. Aidan (himself a student of Columba from Iona.) Chad went on to Ireland for further study after Aidan had died in 651.

Chad's older brother Cedd was sent by King Oswui of Northumbria to evangelise amongst the Middle Saxons, and he had a cell in the ancient Roman shore fort of Othona at Bradwell on Sea Essex. That must also have been close to the border with the East Saxons of Essex. The other two brothers were Cynibil and Caelin (chaplain to Ethelwald, nephew of Oswui) and they helped Cedd to found the Lastingham monastery on the North Yorkshire moors. Chad arrived there in 664 to take over being Abbot from Cedd who has just died of the plague. This was just after the Synod of Whitby, which had decided to favour the Roman model of Christianity.

The plague had wiped out several bishops in England, so a candidate to take the post in Northumbria called Wilfred (of the Roman Christian persuasion) had to go abroad to become ordained. He was there for some time, and the kingdom of Deira (by then a part of Northumbria under a sub-king Alfrid) needed spiritual guidance. So Oswui invited Chad to become a Bishop of York and the Northumbrian kingdom.

Chad also had to find three bishops to ordain him and travelled eventually to Wessex where Bishop Wini of the West Saxons and two Welsh bishops completed the task. Unfortunately, none of them was recognised by the authorities in Rome. In 669 Theodore, a newly arrived Archbishop of Canterbury, instructed Chad to step down in favour of Wilfred, who had finally returned three years earlier. Chad agreed to do so but was ordained a bishop again (this time with the approval of Rome) by Theodore. Chad retired to Lastingham monastery.

The retirement was brief: Only a year later in 670, Theodore recalled him to become bishop to the people of Mercia and Lindsey. Wulfhere donated the land where Chad founded the monastery at Lichfield, and there was another foundation in Lindsey. Mercia covered a vast area by this time. Chad was bishop for only about two years before he died on 2nd March, 672, and was buried at Lichfield. A cult sprang up almost immediately, and some his bones now reside in St Chads Cathedral, Birmingham.

I understand that there are at least twenty-five St. Chad's Wells in the UK, but there is one I spotted on a map (TL933830) long ago that does not seem to be commonly listed. It is just off the A1066 between Thetford and Diss in Norfolk. The location is Shadwell Park, which one could imagine to be a corruption of Chadwell, but that is by no means guaranteed. In essence, early sources indicate Scadewelle as the original form, which I understand could mean 'shallow spring' rather than referring to the Anglo-Saxon saint's name. There is also the Shadwell family locally, one of which was the famous 17th century Poet Laureate and playwright Thomas Shadwell, author of 'Nymphs and Shepherds.'

The nearest existing church at the adjoining parish of Brettenham is St. Mary's, which is apparently rebuilt over a Norman structure and does not have a dedication to Chad. It is said to incorporate some 14th-century material into the tower. The whole place was rebuilt in 1852 but is now unused and currently being repaired. There was an Anglo-Saxon cemetery of about 300 cremations discovered in the parish in the 17th century.

I was disappointed to find on my visit that St Chad's Well is enclosed within the private grounds of Snareshill Hall and the Shadwell Estate, a successful racing horse stud owned by the Dubai royal family. However, I was very fortunate in meeting a charmingly helpful estate worker who took pity and let me see the site. The spring had been enclosed with a small building in the 19th century. In shape, it was in the form of a cartoon igloo, with a stone pillar supporting the dome of the roof, and a delightful archway and steps leading down into it. The walls are studded with local flints but also incorporate some shaped pieces of stone masonry, origin unknown. The spring flowed clean and pure from the wall into a stone basin, which overflowed into a narrow channel on the floor to drain away. The estate worker pointed out that soldiers had left some graffiti on the stone pillar. They were about to be dispatched to the D Day landings in WW2 and were stationed there. Old sources mention that the place was popular with medieval pilgrims on their way to the Shrine of Our Lady of Walsingham.

Some questions remain: was it a well with a connection to St. Chad, and if so, why is it there? One can only speculate, but my thoughts are that Mercia included this area of East Anglia at the time of Chad, in the late 7th century. The ancient long-distance trackway known as the Peddars Way / Icknield Way (running from the North Norfolk coast to Southern England) passes within half a mile. People wanting to have a meeting usually choose a well - known spot on the landscape, and a valued spring of fresh water would be such a place. Therefore, if Chad had come to preach in this area as part of his diocese, it would have been a sensible place to choose. Although there are few houses there now, records show that there was quite a community locally up to about a century ago, needing the now deserted church repaired in 1852. The fact that the church is reputedly built on a Norman foundation suggests there was a population there back in around 1100, also supported by the existence of the Saxon graveyard.

What could possibly go wrong?

"What could possibly go wrong?" is not a very re-assuring question. A catastrophic and violent disaster invariably follows it. Maybe we should be more pessimistic and ask, "What could possibly go right?" and expect a positive outcome to arise from the inevitable cataclysm like a flower from a rubbish dump.

The older UK generation used to talk of 'the Dunkirk spirit' as camaraderie and a sense of community cohesion arising from the darker periods of World War 2. We have our modern equivalents: people showing their humanity, courage and neighbourliness during disasters as wide-ranging as terrorist attacks, fire or flood that are not evident in everyday life. It seems a shame that it takes something wrong happening for a community or individuals to work together for the common good.

Maybe people do good things all the time but are only reported by the media in the context of some terrible incident. Good news seldom makes news headlines, but I am sure that people are kind to each other every day, and I say that as a reasonably cynical pessimist.

Maybe part of the problem is increasing secularism in the West: there is a perception by some not to expect good deeds from a person without a spiritual path, (or of one that they disapprove of). However, good works are not the monopoly of religious people of any persuasion. A money-orientated atheist can just as well do them as a devoutly religious priest.

As more exceptional minds have pointed out, you can rarely change the whole world by yourself, but you can sometimes alter your small part of it. If everyone did that, the small parts may join up and create a better place more organically than some central decree. Pagans are quite used to having an uphill struggle to obtain equality with other religious paths, although progress has been made in the last three decades. Inevitably on a regional basis, they tend to try to look after 'their corner.' Hence there have been environmental campaigning, interfaith discussions and public events that often change not just a situation but others perception of us. It inevitably means that we have to 'go public' at times, which not everyone relishes. Many work behind the scenes who make just as valid a contribution. We have the ability to be 'what could possibly go right?'

The Empty House

Inspired by a deserted dwelling I saw in the Fens near to the Norfolk coast. The marsh was once drained for agricultural use.

The empty house with its windows boarded up
Looks at desolate fen, with a blind man's gaze.
Wistfully remembers chickens pecking in the yard.
Hard living family filling all it's days.

The sedge beds vapour fingers crawl around the door.
Coloured wall clouds with a fungus stain.
Once ordered tiles stretched across the roof
Now part as if to welcome in the rain.

Brooding fens damp-breath crumbles plaster now.
Mice and insects make homes amongst the cracks.
In a few short years, the house will be forgot.
After man's brief stay, the fen can once more relax.

Eel slithers through what was once potato field,
Indifferent feelings, blindly heads to sea.
If the sea walls break, rivers may reverse their flow.
A landscape changed back to what it used to be.

The Speed of Dark

It all started a few years ago, as a conversation in a pub between me and my friend Ian. He was, as usual defeating my arguments with his superior knowledge of science, so I retaliated: "If you are so clever, what's the speed of dark then?" He looked at me, confused. "Has it got one?" he ventured. "It must have," I replied, "if light has a speed." We discussed it for a few minutes until a more critical topic arose: whose round was it? However, I continued to think about it until a few days later, when I made an internet search for the question. Surprisingly, someone had devoted some web pages to the subject. More surprisingly they have since disappeared, probably taken down on the advice of some sinister government department. Since then, I have done a bit of research and experimenting. The results I present in the scientific paper below. An extract of the work in progress was incorporated into my book 'Confidently Confused' (Gruff, 2014), but I now present the cutting edge of my opus.

Background

Nyctophobia (fear of the dark) is most prevalent in young children, but this usually mutates into a fear of light at the adult stage when they become acquainted with electric bills. However, those of a spiritual path may still experience a 'dark night of the soul' when self-doubt challenges their perception of the world, the Universe and the number 42.

Prof. O.B. Vious stated that we could only distinguish light by the absence of dark. Extrapolating from that paradigm, I have reached a parallel theorem 1:

"We can only distinguish dark by the absence of light."

This new law challenges the long-held traditional view by the more boring geniuses of the scientific world that light and dark are inter-related. To them, I would say study the semantics of the common phrase 'after dark' as a synonym for the night. If such light is the naturally dominant energy, why do we not rather say 'after light?'

If then light and dark are different forms of energy, then it may be perceived that they may have different speeds, mass, spectrums etc.

Data

The speed of light has been calculated as 186,282 miles per second or 299,800 kilometres per second, which in laymen's terms is faster than a Heathen can make mead disappear.

Tachyons are hypothetical particles that can travel faster than light, so if dark were composed of tachyons, it would be faster. Since it is unknown what dark is composed of at present, this remains a moot point until some learned authority funds my future research.

Early research

According to Einstein's 'Special Theory of Relativity' (and according to my experiments so far) in our 'real world,' particles can never travel faster than light. Which is just as well: if they did our ideas about cause and effect would be thrown out of the window, because it would be possible to see an effect manifest before its cause. However, that would be very useful for making rune and Tarot readings.

The earliest references to Speed of Dark experiments were by the author Robert Louis Stevenson in his book '*Treasure Island*' in 1883. In it, he details the handing of a black spot from Blind Pew to Billy Bones. This somewhat slow process was due to the lack of knowledge and advanced technology available within the period.

Theory 2

That dark is faster than light: If it were of equal speed, it would merely follow the light which was switched off. Light from the sun takes 8 minutes 19seconds to reach Earth. If the sun suddenly stopped shining (through for example a total eclipse), we would observe its light for that time, and then a beam of the dark would follow it. However, it may be observed that there is no binary cut off point: there is a fading as darkness invades the edges of the light. I would conclude, therefore that it is travelling at a higher speed than light. I will demonstrate this with Experiment 1.

Set of six experiments demonstrated in front of a large number of independent scientific investigators at the COA Gathering, Oxfordshire 2019. (plus a few drunks that found their way in.)

I conducted all six experiments in full protective clothing: bio-hazard suit, goggles, hard hat and gloves. The seminar delegates were kept at a distance and issued with radioactive warning badges as a precautionary measure and asked to sign waivers against claims for injury.

Experiment 1

Delegates were instructed to conduct their unbiased independent trials:

"Tonight, switch off the light or torch in your tent and enter your sleeping bag while you can see how to do so. Time how long this takes you (ideally carried out by an experimental partner) and observe whether the dark conceals the extinguished light before you reach your bag. Report your findings to the conference organisers first thing tomorrow morning. They will be delighted to independently log and correlate your results as they are unlikely to have much else to do at that time of day. Wake them if they are still asleep."

Unfortunately, the results of this experiment were inconclusive: the conference organisers failed to carry out their duties satisfactorily, and some delegates were reportedly distracted by their 'experimental partners.' It was perceived that some even deliberately misunderstood the nature of this phrase which sabotaged the outcome.

Experiment 2

The original experiment planned had to be omitted due to the narrow- minded attitudes of the authorities failing to permit me to use a nuclear reactor or to use double-glazing salespeople as test subjects. A simpler replacement experiment was substituted.

A single light source was directed onto the bald head of a delegate. Others confirmed that the light was reflected away at a different angle. They were then asked to close their eyes and confirm or deny whether they could still see the reflected light. The results were 97% no, 2% yes, 1% confused and asleep.

Conclusion: Applying standard deviation this represents a high proof of evidence that dark hides inside the human body (including the eyelids) thus blocking light rays. This same effect has been confirmed by the use of bright lights over operating tables and dentists chairs: a highly necessary procedure to flush out the darkness before surgery can commence.

Additional information: Just as a light beam can be split into the individual colours of the spectrum by directing it through a prism, T. Dunderhead (2002) suggested that a ray of dark may consist of various shades. He was two millennia late, as archaeologists have now confirmed that the Egyptian pyramids were designed for that very purpose. Recently translated hieroglyphics show that they succeeded in splitting the dark of night into grey, black and ultra-black.

Experiment 3

Two independent witnesses were called upon to verify my observations of a small wooden box. The hinged lid was opened, and they confirmed that light had entered into it and filled all parts of the space inside.

Conclusion: Dark travels at a faster speed than light because it has to exit the box first to make room for the light to enter.

Experiment 4

The room was darkened, and a small torch switched on. A beam of light was observed emitting from the flashlight in a widening beam. The batteries were now taken out of the torch, and the polarities reversed so that a ray of dark was produced. This beam of darkness could not be seen to be emitted, even if the room was brightened.

Conclusion: The beam of dark must be of higher mass than the beam of light since it falls to the floor instead of projecting across the room. Therefore, dark is heavier than light, so the semantics of using the word 'light' for the opposite to 'dark' is correct as it is 'lighter.'

The conclusion is supported by the 'dark sucker' principle, first identified by Cock & Bull (2017). They proposed that a torch is not a light emitter but a dark sucker. When it sucks a line of dark from the air, it allows light to occupy that space up into what is seen as a beam of light. Nutter (2018) achieved a Nobel prize for his work refining the hypotheses and proving that the effect can be better demonstrated with candles: When a candle is lit, the concentration of dark can be seen penetrating the white wick further, making it blacker as the flame of light continues.

Dr.Mathers of Harvard did try to disprove the 'dark sucker' theory but can be rated a 2nd rate scientist from a 3rd rate institute. He made a schoolboy error in the 3rd page of his calculations in the so-called 'proof.' As everyone knows,

$\Omega/53.5 \times \beta$ to the par 2 factorial = 72 $\pi\epsilon$ is a negative, not positive expression!

He probably forgot to carry the 1.

Experiment 5

To explore whether a shadow is a quantity of 'dark' or merely an absence of light.

If we project a high-intensity light source such as a spotlight at the moon or other distant object such as a mountain, a part of it becomes lit up. If we then wave our hand across the searchlight beam, the hand would only be travelling at a few inches per second, interrupting the stream of photons. Yet the shadow cast across the distant object would move much faster than the speed of light. NB. We are referring to 'darkness' not 'Dark Matter', which is a very different thing. Scientists generally agree that the Universe is 80% full of dark matter. The following statement appeared in New Scientist magazine, 7/10/2013:

"If particles of dark matter had never formed the clumps they are in today, they would scurry around space at no more than a sluggish 54 metres per second. The finding is one of the few known values for a characteristic of 'cold dark matter', thought to be the most common type of stuff in the universe."

Conclusion: Since the 'shadow' moves faster and independently from the light, it must be made of dark and not be simply an absence of light. Dark matter must be different to dark or darkness since it moves slower than light.

Experiment 6

The delegates were previously requested to witness an eclipse, and to report what they saw:

Observations: One half of the Moon appears to shine, but it is generally agreed that this is reflected sunshine. We can see this 'light' side of the Moon from Earth.

Conclusion: From this, we can deduce that without the Sun, the moon would be dark all over. Since the dark is more substantial than the sunlight, it sinks into the craters. When the Earth (or another planet) interrupts the flow of sunshine, the darkness can rise from the holes and with minimal gravity can send a beam of dark to Earth. Similar phenomena can be observed on Earth. At sunrise and sunset, dark can be seen pressured into entering and leaving holes and crevices, while in the absence of sunlight dark can rise to fill the whole atmosphere.

Regrettably, we cannot yet measure the speed at which this dark beam travels since it is moving directly towards us, no more than you can tell how fast an arrow is going by lining it up with your eye. (There is a theory that King Harold first attempted that experiment in 1066.)

My old colleague Will Full (2008) theorised that Earth could not send a corresponding dark beam back to the moon because of the considerable escape velocity of 11.186 km/s required due to gravity, as evidenced by the powerful rockets needed to leave Earth's atmosphere.

Experiment 7

A plate with an equal number of dark milk chocolate and white milk chocolate buttons were circulated amongst the researchers. It was noted that after they had all taken one button only, (upon instruction) that many more light buttons remained upon the plate than dark ones.

Conclusion: Dark moves quicker than light.

Future developments:

There have been unconfirmed rumours of the Russians trying to weaponise the dark by releasing artificially synthesised dark from pressurised cylinders on the battlefield. The idea was that they would be able to sneak up on enemies in broad daylight. Reports suggest that they have not yet managed to meet the challenge of creating an outside layer of light to disguise it, and research has stalled.

Since the conference, I have had communication from two delegates concerning their new insights into aspects of the Speed of Dark. I have, of course, followed tradition in claiming them as my own by publishing first.

Summary

Dark is a separate substance to light with a higher mass and density and travels faster than light.

Peer Group Review

Inevitably with any pioneering new work, there is a need for peer group review. The first part of that was supplied by a large number of delegates at the experiment demonstrations. However, I also submit the genuine, independent published view below:

Niayesh Afshordi: Associate Professor of Astrophysics and Gravitation in the Department of Physics and Astronomy at the University of Waterloo, Associate Faculty of Cosmology and Gravitation at the Perimeter Institute for Theoretical Physic (PI)

I believe the speed "of dark" is infinite! In classical physics, the vast darkness of space could be just empty vacuum. However, we have learnt from quantum mechanics that there is no real dark or empty space. Even where there is no light that we can see, electromagnetic field can fluctuate in and out of existence, especially on small scales and short times. Even gravitational waves, the ripples in the geometry of spacetime that were recently observed by the LIGO observatory, should have these quantum fluctuations.

The problem is that the gravity of these quantum ripples is infinite. In other words, currently, there is no sensible theory of quantum gravity that people could agree on. One way to avoid the problem is if the speed "of dark", i.e. the quantum ripples, goes to infinity (or becomes arbitrarily big) on small scales and short times. Of course, that's only one possibility, but is a simple (and my favourite) way to understand big bang, black holes, dark energy, and quantum gravity.

When the sea turned to beer.

Like many exceptional pieces of oral social history, this was first discussed around a re-enactment campfire with my Ealdfaeder friends. Drink had been consumed.

Mention Southwold to many people, and the one thing they know about the seaside town in Suffolk is that it is the home of the famous Adnams brewery, the ales of which have won many prestigious national awards. Brewing has gone on in the town for centuries, and until a few years ago it was delivered around local pubs by dray horses. Sadly, they have been retired since the brewery moved from beside the lighthouse to a larger new site on the edge of town. It was the previous rapid expansion of the brewery back in 1905 that led to a remarkable event in the town's history that has gone down in local folklore as 'When the sea turned to beer.'

The great copper mash tub was connected by a pipe and valve which led to the barrel filling room. As the adman's brand expanded along with the growth in the population of local industries at Leiston, Halesworth and Beccles, a second pipe had to be added on from the main feed to a hastily erected second barrel store. This process was repeated until four separate feeds were coming out of the pipe junction.

One night in August 1905, the inevitable happened: the much -weakened joint gave way during the night and a considerable quantity of beer flooded out and flowed downhill towards the sea. By the time the accident was discovered, thousands of gallons of Adnams beer had formed a top layer to the denser seawater. Delighted summer swimmers no longer minded if they 'got a mouthful' as they frolicked in the sea. Although the weather was calm and tides low, the delicious addition to local attractions soon receded from the sandy beach. An enterprising fisherman rigged up a temporary 'pier' of planks. He charged a halfpenny to people wishing to go and dip a bucket or any other container they could find in the heavenly froth. It became the basis for the later much sturdier Southwold Pier.

Adam's were losing beer and money fast. In those days the nearest supplier of copper piping and valves was in Ipswich, a long days cart ride away, so it was a total of three days before they could make any permanent repairs. Meanwhile, the residents took maximum advantage of the situation. It gave an idea to Samuel Tellar, a local bicycle mechanic and salesman. Together with his two brothers Stephen and Stanley, he approached the towns somewhat primitive sewerage works and made an offer to process all fluid waste for them. Up until then, the works had discharged straight into the sea, but the town council had been making demands for the beach and sea to be kept respectfully clean for summer tourists.

A deal was agreed, and the three engineers rigged up a pump and filtration plant. It was so successful that they could get rid of the majority of unpleasant components of the liquid, leaving just water and alcohol. They had realised that even when the brewery wasn't having a full - scale leak that there was a large amount of alcohol contained within the water used to flush and clean the brewing apparatus. Unfortunately, the brothers could not persuade Adnams to purchase it back from them since the brewery prided itself on making the finest of ales with quality ingredients. Neither could they find a small- scale process to separate the alcohol effectively from the water. Facing ruin, they explored the field further and discovered that the nearest effective operation was in France. The oldest brother Stephen was dispatched to negotiate, having learnt a little French at school. Remarkably he was successful, and soon tanker steamers were docking at the new Southwold pier to export the water/alcohol mix across the English Channel, for it to have flavouring added to make a continental beer. Looking for a unique name and selling point, the French company decided to name it after the three Tellar brothers. Since each of them had the initial S it seemed pointless to list them separately, so the one name and initial was used plus the French designation for a set of three. The product is still marketed today (albeit without the Southwold contribution) as STellar Artois.

Old Glory & the Cutty Wren

An illustrated booklet and CD were produced for the 10th anniversary of the Cutty Wren revival in 2003. They were made in association with BBC Radio Suffolk, Ken May & Old Glory Molly Dancers & Musicians, and the products have long been unobtainable. I am, therefore making the text available here. On Boxing Day 2019 we celebrated the 26th year of the custom's revival.

The Cutty Wren

It is Boxing Day night in the Suffolk village of Middleton, which is not far from Leiston and the Sizewell Nuclear Power Station. A slowly repeated drumbeat is heard from a lone drummer, and from the darkness emerges a sinister-looking procession of people with blackened, grim faces. A chap in agricultural labourers' clothes, who sweeps the way clear for a Lord and Lady, leads them. The Lord wears a top hat and tails, the Lady a bonnet and elegant green gown. However, by the light of the flaming torches held aloft, it may be noticed that the blackened face beneath the bonnet has a full set of whiskers.

Following them, a man bears a pole, with garlands of holly and ivy around one end. The watching crowd, who have deserted their Yuletide feasts and TV, watch in an eerie silence, as a dozen more men follow, with hats and coats to keep out the cold, and heavy boots marking a slowly measured pace. There is a collection of women too, all in black, with greenery around their hats, carrying a selection of musical instruments and, finally, a good many villagers and visitors, carrying candle lanterns. The solemn procession works its way from the village hall, through the main street of houses, a church, post office and primary school, to outside the Bell public house.

Once there, the women form up as a band, led by a melodeon and featuring instruments as diverse as a saxophone and tea-chest bass. The male dancers take control of the car park area in front of the pub. They shed their overcoats to reveal waistcoats, collarless shirts, neckerchiefs and corduroy trousers. The waistcoats are decorated with green and black bows of ribbon, some of which are secured by a badge made from a wren farthing coin. There follows a sequence of East Anglian molly dances, introduced by a character known as the Umbrella-man, and songs about the Cutty Wren.

The crowd of up to a couple of hundred people has a chance to peer into the greenery on top of the pole as it is paraded around with a cry of 'Please to see the King!' Amongst the leaves, they may spot, by the light of a lantern, the beautifully carved wooden wren (carved by Daphne May), which replaces the older custom of capturing a live one. Many will drop coins in the collecting box offered to them by the Box-man. A portion of the money collected each year is donated to local charities. These have included the Long Shop Museum in nearby Leiston, the Print Museum in Beccles, the Marie Curie Cancer Research Foundation and the Southwold Lights. Some of the money is used to defray expenses.

The final dance outside involves the crowd, who are generally pleased to warm themselves up by joining in the jerky rhythms of the molly. Then the wren bearer (which is me) goes into the pub to retell the story of how the wren became the King of the Birds, and four dancers and a musician perform in the very crowded bar, with a dangerously low ceiling, for one last dance.

After that, the whole entourage departs silently into the night, back to the village hall to remove blacking and costumes, and to enjoy some refreshments. I have noticed small organic changes over the decade to the custom, yet nothing major, e.g. only those required to perform inside the pub enter it now, due to the crush of bodies. A lantern-making workshop in the village hall prior to Yule one year has led to some fancy pyramid-shaped lanterns being set around the wren as it stands in the hall beforehand. It is mounted on a wooden stand, bearing a brass plaque with the date 1994, and the symbols for air, earth, fire and water on each side. Each year, before the procession begins, a new ribbon (either black or green) is added to the wren bush. Old Glory tends to learn at least one fresh dance each year to add to their repertoire, so the dancing is always changing.

How it all started.

Back in 1994, I was singing in a traditional Suffolk folksong session in the Plough and Sail pub at Snape. Some of the singers invited me to come along to another session at the Middleton Bell, in a couple of weeks. It was the 'Clocks Back' session held on the last Saturday in October, run by Paul Aldis to mark the end of British Summertime. I told them that I knew something about Middleton, which was that I had read that it used to have a Cutty Wren tradition, the only one I had ever come across in England. They, in turn, encouraged me to tell the landlord about it, to sing the song I knew about it and to tell the story.

It turned out that several of them had formed a molly dance side and thought it would be great to revive the Cutty Wren tradition as well as practising a traditional dance form native mainly to East Anglia. As neither custom is well documented, a fair amount of hard thinking had to be done as to how best to recreate them as authentically as possible, given the limited amount of research information. The result can be seen each Boxing Day night, the traditional day for the Cutty Wren tradition in other countries of the British Isles, as well as the day recorded for Middleton. Old Glory, as they became known, only usually perform the custom on that night, but dance the molly over a two-month winter season.

Old Glory

The idea for of forming Old Glory was originally voiced by four people over tea at the Towersey Folk Festival, Oxfordshire; Ken May, a morris dancer with experience of Cotswold, North West and other morris traditions, Kathryn Aldis, who already played the melodeon for a group of dancers. Her husband Paul, and Daphne, who was later to marry Ken, completed the foursome.

Back at the Homersfield Black Swan in Suffolk, they refined their plans to incorporate some strict rules of dress and conduct. Music would be in the key of C, which is the one used for Suffolk melodeon tunes. Ken choreographed some dances (some of which illustrate a particular local story), in conjunction with chief musician Kate. They tell me that sometimes a tune suggests a dance, and sometimes vice versa. A list of dances and tunes appears in Appendix 2.

Practices would begin in October with the dancing season restricted from November through to January, the traditional winter period for molly. All musicians and dancers faces were to be disguised with blacking. Most dancers would wear agricultural labourers' clothes, except for the Lord & Lady, and the musicians would wear black overcoats in deference to the winter weather. The sole decoration would be black and green ribbons. Someone has since coined the phrase 'Strict & Particular' to describe their style, and I think it very apt (even if it was initially the epithet to denote a form of Methodism!). Old Glory intentionally presents a blackened, grim face to the world, and one of the best-received compliments for them is along the lines of 'You seem so sinister!' There is however much mirth amongst the side outside of performances, but as one of them put it "I take serious enjoyment from the performance." It is noticeable that the word 'performance' is frequently used within the side, as opposed to the more usual term 'dancing out'. Even those dancers who are not participating in a particular dance will maintain a role and stand stiffly focused upon it, so as not to be a distraction to the audience. The side never lets the audience see them blacking up or half in costume, and the blackened faces often fool the closest of acquaintances in the dark.

Dancers and musicians were recruited, and rehearsals have taken place since then on Sunday mornings from the beginning of October at Rumburgh village hall, conveniently adjacent to the Buck public house.

They decided at the outset to restrict the dancing to males and the music to females. They could recruit many more dancers if they changed this policy but prefer to stick to it. Members of the public have been heard to comment that it 'wasn't fair' that ladies were not allowed to join as dancers, but none had mentioned the unfairness of not allowing males to play in the band. The women all wear large swathes of winter greenery in their hats, some of which is collected by the 'Ivy-man' at the Plough Monday celebration in Rumburgh and ceremoniously burnt together with the dried greenery from the Cutty Wren of two years' previous. A green sash is worn over their overcoats.

The side is summoned by a newsletter in Autumn, announcing details of practices and performance dates. Each year's tour has a name such as 'No Fear', 'No Prisoners', 'No Shame', 'No Retreat' etc. The tenth-anniversary tour's name is, aptly, 'No Regrets'.

The first performance was at the Dunwich Ship on Sunday 18th December 1994. In addition to the four creators of the side, Robin Peters, John Barnes, Matthew Robertson, Janet & David Woods and their son Ben were the performers.

The dancing season may be brief but is quite intense and requires a high level of commitment. In 2003 the side attended the massive Pagan Federation National Conference in Croydon at the end of November. This was followed by performances at Rumburgh Buck, Southwold, Snape Maltings, Walberswick (where they have a torchlit procession), Bungay, Beccles and Middleton for the Cutty Wren. The Whittlesey Straw Bear festival, and a Fenland Tour with some other molly gangs, followed in 2004, and they make a second visit to Rumburgh for Plough Monday in January. This is a traditional custom upheld in East Anglia as an agricultural heartland, and one popularly celebrated by molly gangs.

During the last decade, a number of people have passed through the side. Although some leave because of moving away from the area or becoming physically unable to continue, many return as Honorary Members for two social events each year.

One is an informal camping and social weekend in the Southwold area in early summer, which usually includes a knockout boules competition.

The other is a grand feast, held in February. During the evening, members who have completed their first full dancing season will be presented with their wren farthing badge and coloured ribbons. Miscreants who have been spotted smiling, talking to children, smoking in kit or a range of equally heinous crimes are summonsed to the top table to have a hole punched in their membership card. On perpetual recidivist had his turned into a lace doily one year!

I believe these two social events are as much a part of the tradition of Old Glory as that of the music and dance. It is an opportunity to bond socially, learn the side's history and plans.

The level of pride in what Old Glory achieve is enormous, and although most of us are involved in other folk activities, it remains the activity we are most focused upon throughout the year.

Molly Dancing

Molly Dancing is a traditional ritual dance of East Anglia, especially the Fenland area. Before its modern revival, the last times it was seen publicly performed were in Little Downham in 1933 and Littleport in 1934. Russell Wortley noted some details of dancing in Comberton, and Cyril Papworth did the same in Girton. Two particular influences which have inspired the revival of the dance, have been the Rattlebone & Ploughjack LP, by Ashley Hutchings and friends, and a highly committed Kent revival side called the Seven Champions, who have demonstrated their well-rehearsed style at many national folk festivals. Nowadays, the highpoint of many molly gangs' year is the Whittlesey Straw Bear Festival, held near Peterborough each January. Many molly dancers perform and watch others there, alongside various other sorts of folk entertainment and the spectacle of a huge straw bear parading the streets. Details of this event can be obtained from www.strawbear.org.uk

Background to the Cutty Wren Custom.

When I was still at school in the late 1960s, I learnt a folk song. Part of it I learnt from hearing it at a traditional 'Sing, Say or Pay' session, and partly from a play I had to study at school: 'Chips with Everything' by Arnold Wesker, where it was used as a song of protest by RAF conscripts against their patronising officers. It is a fierce song, and one old boy used to stamp his foot for emphasis at appropriate places when he sang it. I have been told it was also used in a Suffolk peasants' revolt of the 1300s against Simon of Sudbury. One version (inevitably there are several folk variants) goes:

1.   Where are you going?
*(Refrain)*Said Milder to Malder
(Refrain) I may not tell you Said Festle to Fose
Going into the woods
Said John the Red Nose *(Repeat last two lines)*

2.   What will you do there? *(Refrain)*
To hunt the Cutty Wren
Said John the Red Nose *(Repeat last two lines)*

3.   With what will you hunt her? *(Refrain)*
With guns and with cannon
Said John the Red Nose *(Repeat last two lines)*

4.   How will you cut her?   *(Refrain)*
With hatchets and cleavers
Said John the Red Nose *(Repeat last two lines)*
5.   How will you cook her? *(Refrain)*
Bloody great brass cauldron
Said John the Red Nose *(Repeat last two lines)*

6.   Who'll get the spare ribs? *(Refrain)*
Give them to the poor
Said John the Red Nose *(Repeat last two lines)*

As R. J. 'Bob' Stewart points out in his excellent book 'Where is St. George?' *(Moonraker Press)* the song has a ritual call and response form, found in many kinds of religious service around the world. The priest asks a question; the congregation say they do not know the answer. Then the priest gives the answer, and the congregation responds by repeating it. The song is also one of a family of English animal exaggeration songs, such as Lambton Worm and the Derby Ram. In each, the size and means of disposing of the animal are immense compared with the real-life status. One does not need a cannon to shoot a wren with, or a cauldron to cook it in.

Later in my teens, I found a brief mention of a Cutty Wren custom being held within living memory in Middleton. I believed for many years that the reference came from a George Ewart

Evans book. He wrote many books on East Anglian oral history and traditions. However, I have never relocated it, and have since been directed to Allan Jobson's book 'An Hourglass on the run' (1959). I read many of his East Anglian books as well around the same time and hadn't always the foresight to note sources of information down. In it he says his grandfather Mr Barham of Rackford Farm, Middleton told him about Cutty Wren in Middleton when he was a boy, back at the end of the 19th century. He said they would go around the village with others on St. Stephens Day. They would catch and kill a wren and fasten it amid a mass of holly and ivy to the top of a broomstick. Going from house to house they sang;

The wren, the wren, the king of all birds
Saint Stephens Day was caught in a furze;
Although he is little, his family is great.
We pray you, good landlady, to give us a treat!

Maybe the variant last line refers to a difference in calling upon a pub.

Additionally, a correspondent has referred me to "County Folklore XXXV11 – Printed Extracts No.2, Suffolk" in which Lady Eveline Camilla Gurdon quotes Gage's "History and Antiquities of Suffolk" Thingoe Hundred footnote pp. xxvii saying 'Hunting the wren on Valentines Day is not entirely out of use.' This was reprinted by Llanerch Folklore Society in 1997.

As a folklorist, I found the references to Cutty Wren in my native Suffolk exciting. The custom does not exist anywhere else in England to my knowledge. It is however celebrated in Ireland, Wales, Scotland and the Isle of Man. In his monumental book 'Golden Bough', J.G. Fraser reports the custom as existing in France also. There are undoubtedly several Cutty Wren songs and tunes. One goes:

We hunted the wren for Robin the Bobbin,
We hunted the wren for Jack of the Can.
We hunted the wren for Robin the Bobbin,
We hunted the wren for everyone.

Old Glory uses versions of all the songs noted here in their Cutty Wren ritual. Central to these is this one, usually referred to as 'The King.'

Joy, health, love and peace be all here in this place
By your leave we will sing concerning our King.
Our King is well dressed in silks of the best
In ribbons so rare, no King can compare.
We have travelled many miles over hedges and stiles
In search of our King, unto you we bring.
We have powder and shot to conquer the lot.
We have cannon and ball to conquer them all.
Old Christmas is passed, twelve tide is the last
And we bid you adieu, great joy to the new.
Please to see the King!

One of the traditional chants that Old Glory use is worth mentioning:

"Eyes to the blind! Legs to the lame!
Pluck to the poor! Bones to the dogs say everyone!"

In Ireland, the Wren Boys (who often include Wren Girls) often appear outside of the Yule period and may bring luck to a village wedding. The famous Irish folk band, the Chieftains, used to take a party of them each year to their Christmas shows in the USA. In a leaflet produced by Old Glory, Michael Blanford gives an Irish explanation for the custom as English soldiers escaping a rebel attack by being woken by a wren pecking a drum. He goes on to mention the Manx story of an Isle of Man singing siren being defeated by transformation into a wren, that was subsequently killed. The feathers were then said to protect the bearer from a shipwreck. Some traditions have a pole decorated with greenery, while others a wooden 'coffin' house to display the bird. One other tale suggests the wren betrayed St. Stephen to soldiers by singing out from the bush in which he was hiding. A common thread between all these tales seems to be sacrifice or risk of death, and the bird appears to take on the mantle of the 'Sacrificial King' quite often.

Although East Anglia is not thought of as a Celtic area nowadays, it once was the home of several Celtic tribes, such as Boudicca's Iceni, the Trinovanti etc. The wren was revered by the Celts as the King of the Birds, and the story of how it came to this is a tale I enjoy re-telling, both at Middleton on Boxing Day, and elsewhere. The Cutty Wren was the smallest bird known to the Celts. ("Cutty" meaning small)

Some swallows returning from Africa told how the animals there had a king. "Couldn't we have one as well?" they asked. The wise owl was consulted as to how one should be selected, and she said that what set birds apart was that they could fly (very wise!) so it should be the one that flew highest. Chattering magpies spread the news of the competition, and a great flock assembled. A small wren couldn't see what was happening, so pushed her way through the legs of the birds from the back. The sharp-eyed kestrel had spotted the eagle flying in from his mountain eyrie. They all knew he was a great flyer but didn't fancy being ruled by one with such arrogant ways. Contestants dropped out, feeling they had no chance against his great wings. The last call went out just as the wren pushed through to the front and stumbled into the starting place. The jackdaws laughed to see such a tiny competitor, but the wren said if no one else would have a go, then she would.

Encouraged by the others, the race began, started by the boom of a bittern.

The eagle took one flap of his wings and was six foot in the air, while the wren had to take a running jump and flap for all she was worth to keep up. The eagle looked down his beak and took two more flaps, which took him to the height of a tree. The wren made a brave effort, cheered by those below who liked a plucky underdog. The eagle decided to finish off the contest there and then and aimed like a dart for the clouds with his big mighty wings. But what was that on his back but the wren, who had caught up and was clinging on grimly. However, the eagle twisted and turned, she was still gripping with her tiny claws, and thus flying higher. The birds acclaimed the wren the king, and the eagle headed back to his mountain in disgust, beaten by brains, not brawn.

In addition to the 'Old Glory & Cutty Wren' CD issued in conjunction with this book (Gruff CD 021) you may like to explore some other recorded interpretations of the songs and tunes:
There is a stirring Cutty Wren song on the CD Time by Steeleye Span (Park PRKCD34)
Look out for 'Hunting the Wren' on the CD Wassail! By John Kirkpatrick (Fellside FECD125)
Four Scots and Irish wren tunes appear on the CD The Day Dawn by Boys of the Lough (Lough 006CD)

A selection of traditional Cutty Wren recordings from Wales, Ireland and the Isle of Man can be found on A Celtic Christmas (Saydisc CD-SDL 417)

Can Hela'r Dryw (Wales), Sheig Y Drean (Isle of Man), Wren Boys of Dun & Wren Boys Song (Ireland) all appear on the CD Spirits of the Past by String Whistle. (Elly Music EMCD 02)

A Wren Medley appears on the Chieftains album Bells of Dublin and its accompanying video.

The Wren

The wren has the Latin name of Troglodytes troglodytes, referring to a belief that it lived like a troglodyte in a hole in the ground. However, they do in fact nest in all sorts of situations, including nests abandoned by other species of bird. It will defend quite a vast territory from other wrens with aggressive song and actual attack, especially if food is scarce.

The story of it being the King of the Birds has resonance in names given to it across Europe: re d'uccelli, the king of the birds in Italian, Winterkonig – Dutch winterking, and the German terms Zaunkonig, Mausekonig & Schneekonig, hedge king, mouse king and snow king respectively. Older names basileus means king in Greek and regulus prince in Latin. This tiny bird, only about 3.75 inches long from beak to cocked up tail, is not always easy to spot, with its mainly brown plumage hidden in foliage, but can more often be recognised by its beautiful song.

The bird is thought to originate in the Americas and can be found in many variations there. Still, just one European Wren can be found in differing habitats across our continent. There are subspecies of European Wren in the Shetlands, Fair Isle, Hebrides and St. Kilda. For a detailed look at the variations and characteristics of the wren, I can heartily recommend 'The Wren' by Edward A. Armstrong. (Shire Natural History, 1992.)

The 1905 Blakenham Mining Disaster

Yet another discussion around the Ealdfaeder campfire brought this obscure aspect of Suffolk history to life.

East Anglia isn't generally known for mining since there are no known useful mineral deposits. However, the discovery of a precious resource on the land of William Nockles in 1904 led to a brief period of localised mining in the area now beside the modern A14 outside Ipswich, Suffolk. Like the rest of Britain, the area was covered in a thick sheet of ice in the last Ice Age. It appears that there was some form of natural disaster: the earth was still settling down, and earthquakes and volcanic eruption were far more frequent. Archaeologists believe that a massive herd of woolly mammoths were exterminated in one such event. They died together with their young who were thought to suckle mothers for a similar period to modern elephants.

William Nockles was not concerned with their fossilised remains. However, by the nature of the freak accident, the nursing mammoth's milk had been preserved in the form of a rich cheese deposit. It was this that William sought to exploit, using local labour to dig down and extract it. Although the initial find had been discovered just below the surface, the workers had to dig up to 20 feet down to reach the main seam. Suffolk soil is remarkably sandy and unstable in the area, yet Nockles seems not to have allowed for much reinforcing of the open cast face where extraction was made.

Whether it was a desire to recoup costs as quickly as possible or an effort to prevent the cheese from being spoilt by wind and weather, the operation worked on a double 12-hour shift system. (9am – 9pm, 9pm – 9am.) Undoubtedly, the face was not that wide, so only a limited number of miners could access it at any one time. Space was tight, and young boys were employed to cart the cheese away in wheelbarrows which they had to steer around the rough terrain. Although children had been banned from mines in the Coal Mines Regulation Act of 1842, it did not cover open cast operations.

It was on the night shift on August 24th, 1905: It had been very hot during the day, but at around 9pm there was thick cloud cover making it quite dark. The miners used tallow candles (which they had to pay for themselves) attached to their hats with wet clay to provide a glimmering light to see their work. They were digging into the already slightly melted deposits with picks and hauling it down into the wheelbarrows. Their sons operated many of these.

The two survivors (John Hewlett and Richard Catchpole) said that there was no warning. A mass of the part - melted cheese (probably affected not just by the day's sun but the heat of the candles) suddenly slumped almost silently on top of the workers. By the time that help was summoned from houses about half a mile away, the victims had succumbed to crushing and suffocation. Twelve men and five boys were killed and are buried together in Little Blakenham churchyard. Nockles insisted that they had been negligent and refused to pay any compensation to the widows. A local parish clerk called Frederick Packman wrote and published a broadside news sheet and a ballad about the disaster. It was sold for a penny, and all profits were divided between the widows.

The mine never re-opened, and Nockles disappeared. His death was later recorded in Lancashire six years later. The workings flooded, but Needham Lakes as it is now known can be seen from the A14 between Ipswich and Stowmarket.

Prog Rock

The music that one absorbs in one's youth stays with you for life, and this is certainly true for me. Having been subjected to the early pop music of the sixties, mainly via pirate radio stations, I became a part-time disco deejay from the tender age of thirteen. In those early days of mobile discotheques, with primitive equipment and no light shows, one hauled around great boxes of 45rpm 7" singles plus a few 12" Long players. You were expected to cover both the Top 20 and popular non-chart dance music, principally soul and reggae.

Consequently, I had quite an eclectic taste and knowledge of pop at the time, aided by TV and an almost religious cover-to-cover reading of the weekly *Melody Maker* magazine. Gradually, rock music emerged from the more commercial material, often played by bands such as *Fleetwood Mac* who had cut their teeth on the late sixties British electric blues boom, spearheaded by the likes of *Alexis Korner* and *John Mayall.* Some went for a 'heavy rock' sound, and all three of the early leaders in that field (*Deep Purple, Black Sabbath and Led Zeppelin*) all also created longer progressive tracks on their albums. Some others explored psychedelia (often with the aid of illicit drugs) which partly led on to prog rock. Others became bored with formulaic structures of songs and the simple use of instruments. They wanted to play to a high standard, (such as Jon Hiseman, the drummer of *Colisseum*) and not to be confined to 3-minute verse/chorus/verse, Moon-June lyrics and 4/4-time signature radio-friendly ditties.

Because of these aims, the movement became known as 'Progressive Rock.' It was music that you sat on the floor in your trench coat, velvet loon pants and tie-die tee-shirt and listened to intently, so it was not so popular with girls who wanted to wear pretty dresses and dance. It required good quality sound systems that could broadcast the subtleties of quieter passages and range of complex instrumentation and sophisticated arrangements.

Some bands started incorporating flutes, fiddles, brass and woodwind. Several (such as *Camel, Greenslade, Nice and Egg*) brought in electronic keyboards to be the lead instrument, rather than the guitar. Some pieces lasted ten or twenty minutes, with several changes of key and time signature. The lyrics may be about mythology, stories from history or whimsical studies of eccentric characters and creatures. Most vocals were very English in content and sound, without the American influence frequently heard in commercial pop music.

Bands also drew on other forms of music to colour their own. *Jethro Tull* and *Incredible String Band* drew upon folk music. *Soft Machine, Osibisa and Gentle Giant* demonstrated jazz credentials. *Emerson Lake & Palmer, King Crimson, Moody Blues, Procul Harum, Barclay James Harvest, ELO and the Enid* all incorporated classical themes into their work. The mighty *Pink Floyd* popularised psychedelia into their early work, and my favourites of the era, *Genesis* (of the Peter Gabriel period) incorporated theatrical presentation within the enduringly popular 'Suppers Ready' multi-part epic.

Record companies jumped on the bandwagon and found that the music, musicians and the fans valued albums rather than singles. Of course, if a track could be released as a single and reach the chart, it would increase album sales and the pulling power of the band as well. E.g. *Argent, Curved Air, Manfred Mann's Earthband, Supertramp, Family & Atomic Rooster*. Album covers became increasingly crucial to selling the music, (since it was unlikely to be heard on the radio) and the likes of Roger Dean became famous for his album cover artwork.

Live appearances developed from specialist clubs such as the UFO in London through the college circuit and into concert halls and festivals. Some bands (such as *Man, Fruup, Egg and Van Der Graaf Generator*) developed enormous live reputations without ever having any major record sales or breakthrough into the mainstream.

I was extremely fortunate in my teens to become a supporting DJ & compere to many major prog-rock bands, especially in my native East Anglia. It resulted in extra income to go to concerts and festivals across the UK. I wrote a music column in local newspapers, enabling me to get into gigs free and interview many leading names. It was a wonderful experience that has influenced my whole life.

Some mainstream artists have produced progressive tracks on their albums while keeping their reputation in other fields. E.g. The heavy metal band *Iron Maiden* recorded an epic track about the R101 airship on the Book of Souls album called 'Kingdom of the Clouds.' 'Bohemian Rhapsody' by *Queen* is undoubtedly progressive, although the band has made almost every kind of popular music. Inevitably, to this day cognoscenti dispute whether some artists such as *Uriah Heep, Kate Bush, Stackridge, Boston, Traffic and Jimi Hendrix* are actually 'progressive.' I think they all are.

Although classic prog. rock has been mainly identified with the UK; inevitably other countries became part of the movement, such as *Focus* from the Netherlands, *PFM* and *Goblin* of Italy and *Rush* in Canada, *Mothers of Invention* in the USA, *Aphrodites Child* of Greece plus a whole movement of electronic music bands from Germany.

The bubble seemed to burst in the late 1970s when the punk rock movement challenged what they saw as dinosaurs with pretentious ideals, over-blown presentation and remoteness from 'the kids.' Music papers turned upon the genre attacking the likes of the phenomenally successful *Yes*, and prog rock seemed to be forgotten by all but the faithful.

Fast-forward to the last couple of decades, and we find a surprising revival: the older fans like me are now generally more able to indulge our passions financially, attend concerts and replace our old vinyl with CDs. Some tremendous old bands such as *Caravan, Gong, Arthur Brown, Hawkwind and Focus* have come out of retirement and are making new albums alongside a newer wave of artists such as *Dream Theater, IQ, Legend, Gandalf's Fist, Marillion, Pendragon, Opeth, Pineapple Thief and Spock's Beard*. Long may it continue!

Hans

A long time ago a poor German peasant boy was walking through a wood when he saw a bottle at the side of the path. Hoping that it was something good to drink, he opened the cap, but to his surprise, an old man appeared to emerge from the bottle.

"Greetings mortal!" he said. "Thank you for releasing me from the bottle. In gratitude, I Hans the Magician will grant you one wish. What is it to be?"

The peasant boy thought hard and long, and eventually said "Thank you kind Hans the Magician. I am a poor peasant boy, so I think that most of my needs could be met if I had a large bag of gold coins."

"That is a wish I can give you. Come closer to the bottle" instructed Hans the Magician. It contains the magic essence of a dozen fairies I squashed and distilled to obtain their magic, which is why I was shut away in the bottle with them." With that, he waved his hand so that a mysterious green vapour passed beneath the nose of the poor peasant boy, who suddenly found that he was holding a large bag of gold coins.

"Oh, thank you very much, sir!" said the boy, but how did you do that?"

"I suppose you are too poor to have a television" mused the magician, "but with your new-found wealth, maybe you will buy one and find out." With that, he disappeared, but later the boy did buy a TV and learnt the wisdom:

Hans that does wishes can waft in your face
With boiled green fairies liquid.

Living as a Heathen in 21st Century Britain

For me personally, life is so much easier now as a Heathen than when I first started to become active in the 1980s. Due to the concerted efforts of a multitude of Pagan spiritual paths and organisations over the last five decades, (including the Pagan Federation of which I was a President), the media are in general better informed and less likely to label us as devil worshipers sacrificing babies and virgins etc. than back in the bad old days of lurid tabloid headlines. I am now less likely to have to explain what we are, and more likely to be asked onto radio and TV shows to give balance to fundamentalist rhetoric.

The UK Government recognises Earth-centred spiritual paths and pays some of us to provide a Home Office chaplaincy service into prisons. Some of us are involved in interfaith dialogue with other religions. This is still a controversial idea to many, but I believe that talking and gaining an understanding of each other is preferable to ignorance and fighting. Some Heathens do not associate themselves with Pagans, but I continue to enjoy intra-faith activities with Druids, Shamen and Witches etc., sharing their conferences, magazines, camps and moots. Personally, I feel that we have more in common than that which divides us.

Yet, it is not all mead and honey cakes. Some folk are still subject to discrimination and abuse within their families, community or even at work (despite the Equality Act 2010, making the latter illegal.) One of how the Heathen & Pagan communities and I have tried to have their presence better officially recognised is by getting the official Census for the various countries within the United Kingdom to include or count Pagan and Heathen categories under religion, then encourage people to record it. Inevitably, some still fear their anonymity will be compromised while others label themselves so finitely as to be counted within a unique class of one!

A partial solution for this has been to persuade people to label themselves Pagan-Wiccan, Pagan-Druid or Pagan-Heathen, etc. Yet such is the individualistic nature of many even this was disputed. Some Heathens do not accept that theirs is a subdivision of the more general Pagan term, unlike Christians or Muslims who are willing to be classed as 'Christian – Baptist' or 'Muslim – Sunni' etc. However, even with those sorts of restrictions on getting an accurate count, there were over 80,000 Pagan related individuals counted in the 2011 England & Wales Census, about double the number reported a decade before. Estimates of the actual figure range from 100,000 upwards, meaning that there are more of us than Buddhists for example, who have always been a minority group recognised by the government. Yet we continue to be a divided group, often suspicious of leaders, organisations and writers within our community, and governmental organisations outside of it. This attitude does not serve us well and often hinders the progress made on the 'divided we fall' principle. A leader who I took over from said it was 'like herding cats' and that still rings true to me.

When I first started reading about Paganism in the 1970s, the choice was minimal: a few good witchcraft books sold from beneath the counter of individual shops like illicit pornography, or sensationalist fiction such as Dennis Wheatley. There was next to no material on paths other than the most popular witchcraft in its many forms. Some books eventually started to filter through from the USA but were inevitably orientated for that country and often quite simplistic. Finally, the UK began to get its literary act together. Still, most of the books were beginner's guides (albeit including Druidry, Odinism & Shamanism) but as an avid reader, I got fed up with the same old material being recycled.

Of course, from a publishing point of view, beginner's books sell best, (and I have written some myself) but eventually there was enough of a mature audience to justify better researched more advanced studies. I applaud the academic

Prof. Ronald Hutton for showing people how it could be done, citing proper references for every statement made and going back to source materials to challenge our own 'sacred cows.'

This new wave of books has enhanced the qualities of talks and discussions within our community. It now includes many books concentrating on specifically narrow interests to deal with them in detail. I particularly enjoy writing in that way now. Since I research and write principally for my benefit, whatever follows in book sales or talks are a bonus.

The most significant difference of all to my life as a modern Heathen in my sixties is the internet. It did not exist when I took my first tentative steps in trying to find others of a like mind. Using pseudonyms to prevent identification by work colleagues or journalists, and moots not yet been invented, it was tough, particularly outside of major cities. Any debates tended to be via slow mail letters or expensive landline telephone calls. Mobile phones were not yet generally available either.

Now I can communicate by email or web forum every day across the world cheaply and efficiently, and access most original texts I want to research from the comfort of my own office. Of course, it does have the downside that instant communication can lack forethought in posting things better left unsaid, and rumours can spread out of control. (I did not die in 2005 – that Peter Jennings was the anchorman for ABC News in the USA!)

Conferences and camps have proliferated: from a couple of small ones in London in the 1980's we are now spoilt for choice, with at least one in almost every county of England and some reaching audiences counted in thousands. As a rural dweller, I love the chance to meet others of a similar ilk and trade ideas and experiences. Otherwise, my path could become a lonely one without fresh stimulus to re-energise it. Those events have inevitably become more professionally run, with a better range and quality of speakers and workshops than their early forbears and I spend a lot of time and energy travelling around to them each year.

Yet, as I look at all the developments I have seen over the last forty years, they are as nothing if I have not developed my insight, ability, faith, connectedness or whatever. I am a human like any other, so I will inevitably fall short of my ideals, but it has been said that no spiritual path has value unless it changes the thoughts and actions of its followers. Embracing what was once termed Odinism or Asatru, or more latterly Heathenry has had several apparent effects on me:

I stopped working in sales and sought out more meaningful, moral, honest and hopefully more socially helpful employment. In my case that involved studying first as a counsellor/psychotherapist and more latterly as a social worker. I developed my interest in history and as a result, became an enthusiastic Anglo Saxon & Viking re-enactor. This has enabled me to get a taste of the cultures in which my beliefs are rooted. I have also been able to pass on my knowledge to the public.

As someone not afraid to live openly as a Heathen, I was encouraged to write articles, then books and lectures. Everyone has something to offer back as a gift to their Gods and Goddesses, and I like to think that my previous abilities as an organiser, entertainer, folklorist, radio presenter etc. have been utilised by my deities to increase their visibility.

Of course, my path has introduced me to many wonderful people who form the bulk of my friends. They are very different from the people I once associated. I am fortunate also that my wife is of a similar path, which gives us some significant interests to take joy in together. To non-Pagans, I guess I appear as a slightly eccentric, larger than life gruffly independent individual who is not afraid to speak his mind.

At a practical level, I tend to support environmentally friendly causes and energy sources, try to shop ethically and locally and act honestly and straightforwardly. That does not necessarily mean that I am a 'good' man, but only that I try to be, and in that, I sometimes fail. It also means that I spend far more time than I ought to on the computer as well as buying and reading loads of books, and I can get quite irate when I see unfair situations.

I can look back to my early writings and notes and see how heavily I was influenced by the then dominant Wiccan methods and ideas. Since then, through combined research and modern translations, we now have a far better idea of what Heathens historically got up to, and what they believed. Hence, I have developed a ritual style that incorporates some of those ancient practises when useful yet acknowledges new methods may be more appropriate for the very different culture I live in today.

I am optimistic about the future of Heathens and Pagans in general in the UK but know that now we are better established we make a bigger, more important target for religious fundamentalists. Both our biggest strength and weakness is our diversity, but I would not have it any other way. As a path that demands that we think for ourselves and establish our truths, we will never have the mass appeal of highly organised religions with powerful officials and text giving absolute answers on a plate. Nor should we ever seek that mass appeal but remain a group of divergent ideas that thinking people sometimes find as useful for themselves.

The Emperors Laws

As my age increases, so does my despair for politics and the world. For years, I have been saying to anyone who will listen (and to quite a few who know better than to do so) "When I rule the world as Supreme Emperor I will ....." followed by some arbitrary law that I will pass to correct the latest bout of insanity that I have had to endure. Some of these new laws are for major issues, others to sort out more practical problems or allow for my private bugbears. Since they have amassed to a fair old bit of legislation over my 67 years, I thought I had better write some down before I forget them with increasing senility. Also, it is just in case the people see sense and replace the government with me, although it is unlikely since I am most influenced by the Patrician in Terry Pratchett's *Discworld* novels. Someone will have to record everything and pass it down to the courts.

The usual criticism made here is that there are already too many laws and an overloaded legal system. My response is that I will make the justice system more streamlined. There will be no trying to decide a sentence, taking into account probation and medical reports etc. since the punishment for almost every major crime will be swift execution within seven days from the date that they are found guilty. With no new inmates, prisons will no longer be overcrowded and will eventually (as existing prisoners are released) become 7-day holding cells for those awaiting trial. This system will also prevent the undesirable possibility of repeat offenders.

All communications between police, lawyers, prisons and the courts would be via secure e-mail, and they can lose those silly clothes and wigs. To simplify matters, and avoid reading and quoting obscure, long-winded documents the existing laws would be replaced by a simple written code taking no more than one side of A4 paper. In addition, I will make the following rules:

1. Small cars banned from car parks where you cannot see them before turning into the space. They can have their own particular area.
2. Advertising may not use any of my favourite music or show unrealistically sized models.
3. Marmite will, in future, be an 'under the counter' product so that ordinary shoppers do not have to see or handle it. There will be a Government Taste Warning on each bottle.
4. There will be dedicated free TV channels for archaeology/history, Paganism, handicrafts, humour and wildlife documentaries. A subscription sports channel will still be allowed but will be subject to interruption or cancellation if important archaeological discoveries are made. Soaps, Quizzes & Reality shows

will all go onto other subscription channels. Stephen Fry will be made the Minister for Entertainment.

5. Censorship will concentrate more on the depiction of violence and less on whether an erect nipple or penis is wrong.

6. News programmes on all media must include positive items as well as the usual menu of death and scandal. News must be factual, without any discernible bias, and stories about entertainers and sports stars are excluded as not being proper news.

7. Arts Council funding will be re-focussed upon the preservation of folk traditions and historical re-enactment.

8. No general public institution or events may include Christian prayers or teaching without an equal amount of input from all the other principal religions. Religion will be banned from schools for children up to 11 years old, and senior teaching will be of a multi-faith nature.

9. The Department of the Environment will in future, be led by environmentalists from a broad spectrum, chaired by David Attenborough.

10. Hadrian's Wall will be required in its entirety for lining up all those I want to dispose of: Blood sports enthusiasts, paedophiles, litter louts, racists, bigots,

tabloid editors, and whoever re-named Snickers bars as Marathons.

I could go on but will not, or the article will run into several volumes. It should at least give a taste of what you could expect from me as Emperor. The problem is, I would probably have to add a law banning myself as Emperor: I don't think I would enjoy a world run by the likes of me.

The Gothi & the rune stave.

This was written initially as a small novella booklet but has long been out of print. I had researched extensively to find the situation of Icelandic people and their beliefs at this period but chose to put the facts into a thriller/murder mystery fictional form.

South West Iceland, Spring of 999 AD.

Chapter 1

A white flag waved furiously. This was not the flag of truce, but that of excitement. It was the curled tuft at the end of the dog's tail and stirred Bjorn from the gruelling walk through the late afternoon gloom and snow flurries. His pace quickened on the frozen Icelandic track to investigate what was interesting the usually docile, thick-coated hound in front of him so much. Slumped into the bank was the dark form of a body, silhouetted against the snow by a crimson backcloth of blood. Bjorn checked for any sign of life, pushing the inquisitive dog away so that it's pointed ears lowered in disappointment. Shaking his head slowly to himself, he straightened, and issuing a curt 'Here!' made off at speed towards his master's hall, still a long seven miles away.

He needed to tell him quickly since the law threw suspicion on any delay. On a more personal note, he was anxious for the fire and food that awaited him there on his return from his elderly mother on the coast, to whom he had delivered a gift of medicine from his master the Gothi, Sven Grimsson. He did have the sense to look for any footprints other than his own, but the recent snowfall had obliterated all signs of activity. The journey had been hard, slippery and cold, in this the Cuckoo month of Gaukmanuthr. He had tramped the long route round from his mother's fish shed on the beach at Thykkviboer near the mouth of the River Thorsa. It was too dangerous to cross the meltwater swollen ford on the River Ytri-Ranga, which led directly to his master's farmstead near Oddi, so he had taken the longer route via the main track from Hilderandi to Selfoss. It was at the junction with that road and his homeward track that he and the dog had discovered the body.

Grimsson had thinning grey hair and a more luxuriant beard. A silver ring could be seen around his right arm that was thrust out of the dark woollen cloak, which flapped against the restraining pin of a circular brooch. He wore a fine pair of leather boots, into which he had pushed the bottoms of his baggy trousers, and these were partially covered by a long blue woollen tunic, worn over a linen shirt. A Thorshammer Mjollnir pendant hung from his neck, but it was his piercing blue-eyed gaze that registered with Bjorn most as he approached the yard in front of the hall. Grimsson growled,"

What is it?" at the panting nervous man he saw before him. It wasn't that he was particularly unkind, just that in his fifty years of experience he had found that appearing stern sometimes got the best and most truthful results. With some hesitation, the man recalled in vivid detail what he had seen. "Did you recognise him?" the Gothi asked. Bjorn shook his head. "It is dark now. Tomorrow morning you had better lead the housecarls back to him so that they may fetch the body on a cart." Grimsson's wife Aud hovered serenely nearby. Looking up and nodding to her, he added: "You'd better get some soup and ale into you."

She felt a little sorry for the man. He was a good and hardworking servant, but short in stature and lacking the self-confidence of his companions. She knew of his concerns for his elderly mother, and love of fishing, but not much else. He usually just got on with his job and tried to avoid being noticed. He was about to become the centre of attention, which must be quite disconcerting for him. She led the now shivering man away, but returned, with some fermented honey mead for her husband and self. It was their favourite time of the evening when the day's work was done and over; the evening meal had been finished. Grimsson looked up at her approaching alerted by the faint clink of the house keys that hung on her belt, a very practical badge of her high status as head of the household. The peat fire glow extended to the amber beads she wore, hung between two brooches on her bosom. He smiled and patted the twin high seat to the left of his, grateful for his wife's company and advice in most matters.

The Hof hall was a long rectangular building, with the twin seats set against the middle of one of the longer stone walls, opposite to the main entrance door. The peat fire burning in the middle sent a stream of smoke to permeate through the mossy turf roof. It illuminated the raised platforms dimly along each wall, where tables and benches were set up, and the old sword buried almost up to the hilt by an ancestor into the central upright support beam. Turning to his wife, Grimsson announced his intentions. "Since the man is dead on my land, my duty is to investigate it. The Althing Council is soon, and they will want to know everything when I attend." Aud nodded and quietly added, "I suppose there will be some who will try to make it look bad for you, whatever the reason."

"No doubt!" he retorted. "Getting the Witan Council to adopt the new Christian religion is still not a forgone conclusion. There are still some of us true to our older Gods and Goddesses. They will stop at nothing to discredit us, yet it is they who show discredit by their lack of faith in those who protected our forefathers and us! I don't mind them worshipping whoever they like really, so long as they leave us alone to follow our old traditional ways."

"I know, but we must be careful – they are quite powerful now, and our neighbours on each side are part of their number. Do not upset yourself my great bear."

Embarrassed by her use of a secret eke name (or nickname) in possible earshot of others he turned away and barked at his group of half a dozen young housecarls, who were playing or watching a noisy board game of King's Table in the corner. They shuffled forward to him immediately, anxious to please when the old man was not in the best of moods from the servant's news. "Get out there early in the morning to bring the body back here. Take a hound or two to seek it out in case it has been covered by the snow, and Bjorn to show you where he reckons the body lies. Keep an eye out for any strangers and ask the old shepherd Njal if he has heard anything. He doesn't live far off the track."

With that, he turned and strode through to his small private bedchamber. Aud followed, dropping back the hide curtain that separated them from the main hall, and fulfilling her last wifely duty of the night by pulling off his boots. Beneath the bearskin covers she lay, but sleep did not come readily when your husband tossed uneasily, mulling over the problems of the day.

"The foolish man lies awake all night
And worries about things;
He's tired out when the morning comes
And everything's just as bad as it was"

she whispered. A grunt and a snort was all the reply she got, but he rested easier with those words of the Havamal verse in his ear and drifted off musing whether having a wife educated in the sayings of the High One was such a bad thing.

It would be several months before the long days of full light, but the half dozen young men who formed the housecarls were roused and ready to go early next morning, having rapidly eaten some gruel for their davre, the morning meal. They chided Bjorn for keeping them waiting. Here was something a little more exciting than their employment on the farmstead, which seemed a much larger part of their work than acts of bravery in a war band, for which they were kept in readiness and training.

It was five years since Grimsson had joined a raid against the Saxons, and he didn't seek strife with his neighbours either. Of the young men, only Rolph had been old enough to accompany him on the raid. The most violent action they ever saw seemed to be the occasional ball games of knattleikier. The others here had replaced the older men who had since left him. Some had married and were tenant farmers; one was now aboard a Viking raiding ship while one had died in battle and was probably taken directly to the warrior heaven of Valhalla by the Valkyries.

Grimsson was respected for his fighting skills, which he was glad to pass on, but at fifty years old was sometimes referred to as the 'Old Man' by his less respectful men, when they were sure he could not overhear them. They covered the seven miles to where Bjorn indicated quickly, hanging onto parts of the horse-drawn wagon that occasionally slithered on the icy track. No more snow had fallen overnight, and the spring thaw was already showing its evidence in the puddles of water that formed in the ruts in the cart track. The corpse was relocated, and a silence fell upon them as they gingerly lifted the frozen pathetic bundle onto the cart. After turning the cart around, none seemed keen to share it with its dead passenger, and it was left to Bjorn to drive it home, the rest following on foot alongside or behind with a subdued air. On the way, they saw Njal, the shepherd, but he had seen or heard nothing in the area.

Grimsson could be seen with his hand to his brow against the low sun, standing in the yard beside the entrance to the farmstead. With agility that defied his weary look, he sprung onto the tail of the cart as it stopped. "Anyone know him?" he demanded, examining the body.

"I think he is one of Arnason's men" replied Rolph. "I am sure he led his stallion at the horse fight last summer. I think he is bondsman anyway, by his thin clothes." Another one of the housecarls, Atli agreed, adding, "I am sure his name is Erik Snorsson."

Grimsson thought for a moment, and then decisively ordered the pair to carry on with Bjorn to Arnason's land and to deliver the corpse with an explanation of what they knew. He knew that Arnason would wish to question Bjorn and did not wish him to face it alone. Before they left, he checked the contents of the man's purse, hanging from a bloodstained belt. There was a single coin in it, a simple bone ring and a piece of wood. Lines were scratched onto the flat piece of wood, which was about a handbreadth long by two finger widths broad. Without giving anyone else a chance to see the detail, he thrust it in his belt and returned the rest of the contents to the hide purse. There was also a small knife on the man's belt, the blade of which appeared quite clean and polished. "Take some food for the journey. You will need to stay overnight by the time you get there" he added. "Mind you behave as honourable guests, and do not be drawn into speculation or argument, or you'll have me to answer to as well as Budli Arnason!"

Gudrun, his daughter, handed up some flat unleavened bread with bran inside, which had been baked that morning on an iron skillet, together with some cheese and a stone jar of water. She was a striking girl of seventeen, with many admirers of her beautiful long blond hair, ready laugh and curving form. In an earlier life, she had been equal to her male peers in archery and stave fighting, but now she was filling her expected role of weaving, brewing and cooking. With the food safely stored, Grimsson nodded to Bjorn, who urged the horse on. Rolph and Atli jumped up beside him for the day's journey, which they both preferred to spend away from the company of the red-stained passenger in the back of the cart.

Aud followed her husband at a discreet distance into a corner of the hall by the doorway. He was already holding the piece of wood to the light and mouthing sounds under his breath. "It must have been an important message to have sent the man on such a long journey alone at this time of year" she ventured. "Important enough for him to be killed for it, though?" he muttered almost to himself. "If it was so important, why didn't his murderer take it? It was no thief who killed him – a ring and a coin were still in his purse. He had been stabbed upwards to the heart just below the ribs. It was not a large wound, so probably it was made by a dagger rather than a sword or spear."

"Maybe it was a feud. Was he killed over an argument, or in revenge for another's life?" Aud asked, suppressing an involuntary shudder.

"Unlikely, but possible. People who carry on family feuds usually declare what they have done at the nearest village, and are proud of it, and do not get accused of murder. If it was a personal feud, the fellow was hardly likely to expose himself to extra danger by venturing away from his master's land and protection. He had not drawn his knife, so if he saw his killer coming, which is likely with a wound to the chest, he was not on his guard beforehand. He couldn't have thought the person approaching a threat until his dying moments, so maybe he knew him. The murderer would have had to have got close to him to deliver such a wound." Breaking off with a low whistle, he had finally deciphered the last of the runes inscribed into the wood, but to Aud's annoyance showed no sign of reading them to her. She was too proud to ask, so stalked off to issue orders for the evening meal, reflecting sourly that men could be so precise about killing, yet utterly useless in doing the task she was about to undertake.

Chapter 2

"What's this?" was the fierce greeting at the farmstead of Budli Arnason near Selfoss. He stood glowering at them, his chin thrust forward, accentuating the point of his beard, with a group of tough-looking men at his back. The settlement's dogs sent up a howling chorus of alarm and excitement. He was a tall, confident man, proud of being a descendant of Iceland's' first settler Ingolfur Arnason three centuries before. It was in the Reykjavik area, the name of which means 'Steamy Bay' after the mists that gather there. Budli's light coloured hair, good fur cloak and a quizzical brow made an immediate impression. After a brief pause, while they and the waggoners took each other's measure, Rolph spoke up. "Bjorn here found this man dead, on the side of a track. I think he is your man, so we have brought his body straight away. Our Gothi Grimsson says he will investigate since it was on his land.

"You'd better come in and talk" was the reply. "Take the body to the outhouse and prepare him for burial" he added tersely to his men, adding "And the rest of you get on with your work!" They scattered.

"It is obviously a stab wound," exclaimed Arnason as soon as they were inside. Atli nodded, "Yes, the Gothi thought so to." Rounding on Bjorn, as someone less confident and nervous he said, "Tell me all you know and hold nothing back. Under his furious gaze, and with an encouraging nod from his companions, Bjorn falteringly related what had happened, with additional comments from Rolph and Atli, and further pointed questions from Arnason. Turning to Bjorn's comrades, he questioned them also at length. Finally, Rolph tentatively asked whether it was known what the man had been doing, or why he should have been on the track by himself. "I will ask the questions here" roared Budli Arnason. "And I am not satisfied with your explanation" he blustered. "Have some food and drink and sleep here tonight by all means, but tomorrow you can get back to your master and tell him I will want answers to my satisfaction at the Althing Council. It should be dealt with there, not at the regional folkthing. The man Erik Snorsson was a trusted servant, and I will be hard-pressed to find another like him. Now keep out of my way while I see to his funeral arrangements."

The trio made themselves scarce and busied themselves, ensuring the horse was being looked after, as well as admiring the many other beautiful horses in the stable. They were amused to see someone carry nail-clipping tools to the shed where the dead man lay. Cutting corpses nails was an essential part of their own religious beliefs, but they wondered whether their newly Christian host would approve of his servants' actions in clinging on to old customs. It was said that a dead man's nails would form the ship that would bear the evil Loki at Ragnarok when most of the gods would be destroyed.

People started to drift towards the hall for the evening meal, and the smell of stew overcame their reluctance to face further questions. They took care to sit at the far end of the tables, near to the draft of the doors, thus avoiding the likelihood of being accused of taking too higher place above anyone else's regular position. It was a much larger household than their own. Through the smoke of the peat fire at the centre of the hall they could see at least a dozen well-dressed housecarls, plus many more servants and slaves. Clearly, their host had grown wealthy through his trading with Norway. He sat in deep conversation with his wife and son, seemingly oblivious of the general clamour of his servants and guests. His son then stood up, and there was silence. Holding his hands aloft, he said, "Great God, and Son of God who hung on a tree for us, thank you for this food." The throng joined in with the word "Amen." This was the first time Rolph and Atli had experienced what the Christians called 'grace' and coincidentally had the same thought in each of their heads; This son of God sounded just like their Odin hanging on the Yggdrasil world tree, wounded by his spear to gain the knowledge of the runes. Atli had one additional thought: whichever way you look at it, runes are trouble!

A thrall banged wooden bowls in front of them, which mainly contained stewed vegetables with the merest hint of the meat being enjoyed higher up the tables. They kept their heads down and ate with their personal wooden spoons, but as the meal finished their neighbours at the table who had not been privy to their previous interrogation started to ask them to repeat the story. In between comments and interruptions, they answered truthfully but briefly. However, Rolph managed to ask the odd question back to a man who seemed to have drunk more ale than the others had. "The man who died – did he have enemies or was he well-liked?" he probed.

"No, he was alright" was the reply "and well-liked enough by the master to be trusted on his errands. I had a drink with him just a couple of days ago, and he was cheerful then.

"So, was he on an errand when he got killed?" asked Rolph.

"I wouldn't expect Arnason to tell the likes of me his business. If you want to stay healthy, you'd better not ask so many questions either" he snarled, his face suddenly leering much closer to his inquisitors'. The snarl incorporated a veiled threat in the sure knowledge that this man of superior rank had no power over him in this place. Rolph was about to physically rise to the bait though until he felt a firm restraining hand on his arm from Atli. Backing down, he muttered something about 'having to be away early in the morning', and the three left to sleep in the stable, their weapons close to hand as they lay in the straw.

They left very early the next morning, before many folk were about, and took some of last night's bread with them to sustain the journey back. They also had the stone jar of water they had replenished the day before and set off quickly with the horse and cart. They feared in case Arnason should change his mind and want to question them again or even keep a hostage. However, they travelled back the thirty miles with no more incident than a snow shower to their master's farmstead near Oddi, which was overlooked by the brooding presence of the nearby volcano Mount Hekla. Willing hands took the horse to stable, whilst hot broth, served by Gudrun warmed them. "Tell me all you saw and heard" was Sven Grimsson's instruction, which they were glad to do in the reassuring familiarity of their own hall. At length, he praised them for doing their duties but asked them to repeat the conversation about how the victim was regarded. "Do you think he might have been on an errand for his master?" he asked.

"Quite possibly" replied Atli. "I cannot see that he would be let to go wandering around another man's land by himself for no good reason in this weather."

"There is also the way Arnason answered our question with a challenge. Why didn't he wish us to know unless the journey was secret?" added Rolph.

"You make a good point Rolph" replied the Gothi. "The best form of defence is often attack, as I have often taught you" he grinned. "Well done – now go and get yourself warmed and dry." Relieved to be dismissed they hurried away, with tales of how good their neighbour's horses looked for their friends.

The Gothi wandered through the great hall doorway, running his gnarled fingers over the elaborately carved posts. They had been brought from Norway by his ancestor, who had pitched them over the side of the boat in sight of land and made his settlement in the area they were washed ashore. His faith in the guidance of the Gods was absolute, and Grimsson wondered what he would make of the situation today, or what advice he would give his descendant. Sighing, he stepped into the fresh, chilled air outside, aware that his wife was leaning within earshot around the corner of the doorway. She stepped forward, trying to appear calm, but with anxiousness in her voice.

"What do you think it all means?" she asked, not really expecting any explanation.

"I don't know," admitted her husband, "but I'm fairly sure that the man was on an errand from Arnason. If he was having a drink with that man in the hall only a couple of days before, he must have set out from there to reach my land the other night. He could not have been returning to his master."

"Which means the rune stave was almost certainly sent by his master, to someone living the other side of our land" his wife reasoned. "The most likely person would be Bragi Hogni, wouldn't it? They are allies in wanting the new religion officially adopted. Are you going to tell me what the rune stave says?" she blurted out, in frustration in not having all the details of what had happened available.

"I suppose I must. We should not have any secrets as husband and wife, and certainly not with you as my Gytha priestess as well. Still, I didn't want to worry you unnecessarily" he replied, slightly shamefaced for forcing her into confronting him. He took it from the safe place in his belt bag and read it aloud. He hardly needed to examine the row of straight-line symbols, reading from right to left, because he had so often looked at them and considered their meaning in the last days. They had been hacked out of the wood quite roughly and stained with a red pigment, but there was no mistake in their message. "It says 'Bragi – kill Grimsson before the Althing. He is the main obstacle. Budli' he pronounced."

Aud gasped, the colour draining from her face, her hand shaking as she clutched the arm of her beloved Sven. With a tremor in her voice, she asked, "Can it be true?" without any expectation of a negative answer. After she had regained her composure, the Gothi lead her away from the building to the edge of the pigpen, where they could not be overheard.

"It seems that several people may have had reason to kill Erik Snorsson" started Grimsson. "Maybe he had a personal enemy who killed him, but it seems unlikely. He seems to have been well-liked, and an attacker would have had to have known when and where he was going. He would also know that revenge by Budli Arnason would be swift, effective and deadly. You wouldn't sit out in ambush on nights like these on an off chance, and robbery does not seem to have been committed. A coin and ring were in the man's purse as well as the rune stave." Turning the rune stave in his hand to the light he paused, cocking his head on one side and squinting at it once more. It was the first time he had looked at the object in direct sunlight, having kept it away from the prying eyes of other folks up until now. Aware of his wife's look, he recommenced the opening of most of his thoughts to her.

"Arnason and a few others may have known he was travelling. I suppose Arnason could have changed his mind about the message, but surely wouldn't have to kill him to stop him delivering it. Anyway, from past experience at the Althing, I wouldn't expect him to change his mind once he has made a decision." Aud nodded, although she had never been to the Althing. Women landowners were allowed there, just as they were allowed to own property and divorce, but she was only ever likely to attend as a widow. She shuddered at the possibility.

"Alternatively, someone at the receiving end may not have wanted the message to reach Bragi Hogni. Maybe I have friends there. I don't know about who are trying to protect me!" He grimaced a false smile.

"There is one other possible source of the attacker" his wife replied.

"You mean my own men? Unlikely, since they wouldn't know his message or whereabouts. Haven't they all been in the hall these last few weeks anyway, except Bjorn, who has no reason to kill the man? I don't think he can read the rune stave either, or even knew of its' existence before I found it."

"Well, there has been no good reason for anyone else to stray from the fire these last few days. I will ask the servants anyway," added Aud, glad to have something positive to contribute.

"Thank you. I'll ask my housecarls directly, since they would be the ablest to make an attack, maybe from a sense of loyalty if they knew what the message was." They both strode purposely to their tasks but were still acutely aware of the genuine threat to Sven Grimsson's life, from a force far superior to anything that he could muster.

Aud moved amongst her servants and slaves quietly but efficiently, giving each individual the chance to speak individually without being overheard by others. All claimed that as far as they knew, everyone had been at home this last week, except Bjorn who had been given leave to visit his mother.

Sven Grimsson was a little less subtle. He lined his housecarls up in the hall, and fixing them with a stare that had terrified more than a few enemy warriors asked: "Have any of you been away from the hall in the three evenings before the body was found, apart from to relieve yourselves?" All shook their heads, glancing sideways to see if another had. The Gothi knew his young men well, and that they would not betray each other, but sensed the uneasiness between them. "I will not be hard on any man who is truthful!" he encouraged. Still no admission. "In that case, I will ask you all to swear on my holy oath ring, that you had not left the hall in the three nights before Bjorn found the body. May Vor the Goddess of oaths take a terrible vengeance on any who makes a wrongful oath."

So, saying, he took off the twisted silver torc ring from his right forearm, and stood in front of Rolph, at the end of the line. Rolph stretched his right hand to it, and simply said, "I swear." Inevitably, his close friend Atli was standing next to him and copied his action. Sigurd and Giuki swore upon the ring before he came to Hamdir Gettirsson. He froze and did not stretch out his hand. His comrades, including Sorli at the end of the row, leaned forward to look at him anxiously. He shook his head and finally said, "I cannot take a wrongful oath."

Stunned, his Gothi stared at him. Mustering his last bit of confidence, he stood still and looked straight ahead. "Uncle Sven, I cannot swear such an oath, but I do swear this oath, that I know nothing about the murder. Please believe me I would have done the honourable thing and reported it straightway if I had, whatever the cost in fines or exile." He leant forward and touched the ring, still in front of him. To himself, the Gothi thought that this was probably true. He had been an excellent man since being fostered with him by his father the Berserker warrior Grettir Onundarson. It was the right way for young men to learn adult skills away from their own home, and forge lifelong links with their fellows. From the end of the row, Sorli interrupted his thoughts by placing his hand on the oath ring and swearing on it that he had not been absent.

"What were you up to when you left the hall then?" quizzed Hamdir's master.

"I am sorry I cannot tell you" he replied.

"Then we will both think about it overnight, while I ponder what to do with you" Instructing the others to guard him closely in an outhouse overnight, the Gothi went to his private chamber and flung himself on the bed, face down. His mind was turmoil. Whatever the lad said now, he would be a prime suspect and a marked man to Budli Arnason. It would not take long for the story to reach his ears. A little later his wife joined him and tried to tempt him to eat with a favourite dish of salted herrings and pork, but to no avail. He lay and stared into space for a long time, then abruptly got up and marched out of the chamber without saying a word.

He needed the clear night air and a view of the stars. He faced North, towards the uninhabitable volcanic centre of Iceland. "Odin help your Gothi priest," he asked earnestly. "Please give me clarity of thought, to know the truth." Disturbed in its slumber, and unseen in a nearby tree, a raven cawed. "Thank you!" he shouted a reply into the night. It was believed by many that two ravens flew at Odin's command. They were called Huggin and Munnin, and their names meant thought and memory. He took this as a sign that he would have help. Back in their chamber Aud pulled the fur covers up around her, but it was not the cold that made her shiver.

Chapter 3

Gellir Thorstein was splitting some logs into planks with an axe and wedges when the Gothi approached. The clean smell of pine resin was on the morning air as he straightened his back, pushing his hands into the small of his back.

"We all get a twinge or two as we get older," said Grimsson gently, looking tired from his nights wandering.

"But I can still do my work as well as ever" protested Gellir defensively. He was often worried that a younger, more vigorous man might supplant him. Still, Grimsson knew full well his experience produced better results through working at a steady pace than some younger man trying to impress with speed and making expensive mistakes with valuable timber. "Of course, you work as well as ever. I value your carpentry and knowledge, which is why I have come to see you. How is it going with those new mead benches?" enquired Grimsson, wishing to put his nervous servant at ease. He had already spotted a pile of finished, smooth planks, but let the man show him, knowing that he would be put at ease by talking about his favourite (if only) topic of conversation. He let him ramble on for a bit, before extracting the rune stave from his pouch. He showed it to him with the rune side away from him. "What do you make of this wood?" he asked, casually. The man stretched out his hand, and Grimsson passed him the piece of wood. It was unlikely that he would be able to read the runes anyway. Gellir showed some excitement. "This is exceptional wood!" he said. "Are you getting a supply of it?"

"I am not sure" replied Grimsson. "Why is it so special, though?"

"It is the stuff that Leif Ericsson brought back from Vinland, the land he explored over the ocean. They call it red oak, and they say there is lots of it for the taking there. Not only is it cheaper than bringing in pinewood from Norway, but it is also much harder because of its' closer grain. He took some back to his father Erik the Red in Greenland but sold the rest to Bragi Hogni at a good price I hear." (Grimsson remembered Erik the Red well as a tempestuous man who had been exiled nearly twenty years ago at Thorsnes Thing for three killings.) "My friend there showed me some. He says it is marvellous to work with, and Hogni is reserving it for only specific jobs until he can get some more. I expect this small piece is just an offcut leftover from some work. The tree does not grow in Iceland, though. I think it must need a warmer climate."

"You are sure of all that?" said Grimsson, adding, "It is important that I have the right information."

"Oh yes, there is no mistaking it – red oak from Vinland. It is very different from the pine trees and birch we have here in Iceland or those in Norway and Denmark." For the first time that day, Grimsson permitted himself a smile. "Thank you very much. I knew I could rely upon you to know about timber."

Gellir went back to work with a will, as the Gothi walked away with a spring in his step. So lost in thought was he that he nearly crashed into his wife, who was hurrying around the corner to find him. "I'm not sure what it is, but our daughter is distraught, and wants to talk to us both."

"Very unlike her" he commented, as they moved towards the women's quarters. It was a place that he would not usually visit. She had a tearstained face and distraught looks that gave evidence of a sleepless night. Her mother sat down beside her and put an arm around her shoulder in reassurance. "What is it?" asked her father in a gentle tone as he could muster. He always felt inadequate around wailing women. Slowly, she sniffed back her tears, and took a deep breath and turned her head to look at each parent individually. She had rehearsed some words in her head, but they seemed inadequate now she had to speak them.

"Father, Mother. You know that I love you both very much and have always tried to be obedient to you. You have taught me to act with dignity and honour, and yet I feel that I have neither here this morning." She paused, and her parents murmured encouragement, though perplexed to which point she was leading. "I know that Hamdir Gettirsson is being guarded because he will not say where he went when he left the hall the other night and is under suspicion of murder. He will not speak because he is honourable. I cannot be dishonourable by letting him be accused. Oh, Father, he was with me!"

Her mother had half guessed as a woman what was coming as she spoke, but still, let out a gasp. Her father was thunderstruck. His face went red, and he struggled to find the right words or any words for that matter. Eventually, he stammered "W-What happened? D-Did you lay together?"

"Certainly not!" his daughter flashed indignantly. "You both taught me to be a better daughter of Gothi & Gytha than that. If you must know, he read me a poem which he had written."

"Was it a love poem?" her father asked anxiously. "Your honour would be almost as much affected by that. The law recognises the power of love poems and punishes for their illegal use" he added somewhat needlessly. It was well known. His wife smiled a secret smile to herself, remembering his indiscretion in that matter when they were young, and the irony of him being a Law Speaker now. It involved memorising large sections of the oral law built up in the seventy-odd years the Althing had existed.

"No love poetry," said Gudrun, a little regretfully. "It was about his father's exploits at the Battle of

Maeldune, and the raid on Gippeswic. You were in it too. He admires you a lot, you know." Her father remembered the events vividly, from eight summers past. He had fought side by side with Hamdir's father Grettir Onundarson until the man had summoned a Berserker battle rage, for which his warrior cult was famous. It had been terrifying enough to see his old friend transformed by the frenzy, to say nothing to the effect it had on the Saxons defending their territory of the South Folk in the area settled by the East Angles. They fell like corn to the sickle as the warrior had whirled about him with an enormous battle-axe; seemingly impervious to any injury aimed at him. Grimsson's reverie was disturbed by his wife's voice. "Do you love him?" she asked. Her daughter nodded.

"Yes, and I believe that he loves me. He knows that it is no use presenting himself as a suitor to you until he has proved himself and got land of his own."

"Well, he will not prove himself by breaking trust with me" snapped her father, "although it is good, he tried to protect your honour, even at his own cost." He sunk his head in thought, and the women knew better than to disturb those thoughts right now.

Finally, he rose and left without a word. Aud took her daughter silently by the arm, and led her to a jug of water, and dabbed at her face with a cloth, as if she were still a small child, although clearly from what had been said she was not. She combed her hair as well, with the finely carved antler comb that had been a present to Gudrun from her father only last Winter's Night feast. It was hard to know what to say. She wanted to guide her daughter but knew that too stronger words would be likely to put up her defences, and back her into a corner of acting the opposite way. Finally, she broke the silence between them. "Remember that you are a Viking woman of good breeding. Ignore any jibes that come your way if this becomes common knowledge. Be proud that you acted honourably, and grateful that Hamdir kept troth towards your reputation. Not all the men that Lofn the love goddess sends are so noble! You might like to think about making an offering to her and Freyja for guidance and help." It was hard acting the Gytha priestess at the same time as being a mother, and Aud left her daughter to contemplate the outcome of her deeds. A string of contradictory thoughts flooding her daughters head showed quite openly on her troubled face, as her mother strode resolutely away, hoping she had said the right things and making her silent prayers to the Goddess for guidance and help.

Gothi Sven Grimsson was not in such a spiritual mood as he crossed the frozen yard to the outhouse where Hamdir was being held. Dismissing the guards brusquely so that he could talk to him alone, he entered the dim storeroom. It smelled of the salted fish and bacon that had been kept there. With winter nearly over, only a little of the store put by to see them through it was left. Hamdir rose to his feet in respect as the older man entered the small room. Without a word, Sven crossed directly to him and struck him with his fist on the chest. Such was the swiftness and force of the blow that Hamdir staggered back and fell to the ground, groaning slightly. "That was for betraying my trust and courting my daughter without permission!" shouted his attacker. "Now get up!"

The younger man got warily to his feet, and the Gothi was pleased to see him initially adopt the defensive, sideways crouching stance he had taught him. But then he straightened and turned to face the Gothi, with his hands loosely at his sides. "I deserved that", he said defiantly, "and I will make no defence if you want to hit me again, but please do not hold it against your daughter. She is a fine woman whom I love, however unworthy I am."

Grimsson glowered at him for what seemed many heartbeats, then gave a snorting laugh. "You should know me better than that. You did not have any choice as an honourable man to refuse to take a false oath or to stay silent about my daughter. You should not have compromised yourselves in the first place, though. I suppose this leaves you proven innocent of one charge but guilty of another." The housecarl looked enquiringly at him, not noticing the sly smile of his master silhouetted by the light from the doorway. Grimsson, relishing the joke at the young man's expense, slowly explained. "My daughter confirming you were with her suggests you were not out murdering Erik Snorsson. However, the way you went down from that single punch suggests you haven't learnt a thing I have ever told you about being on your guard at all times!" He roared with laughter, and the light dawning on Hamdir, he chuckled to, before wincing at the renewed pain it caused in his ribcage.

Putting his hand out, Grimsson said, "Now let that be an end to it." As they grasped each other's wrists in confirmation of their friendship though he added: "but you will not repeat this action, and I will not accept you as a suitor until I am satisfied you are worthy of her." This was said hoarsely into Hamdir's ear, who nodded vigorously and felt dealt with very leniently by the man whom he respected even more now. Leading him outside, the Gothi told him

"You stink of that place. Get yourself cleaned up, and then get about your work. You will say nothing to anyone, including your friends here, as to what has happened. You are not in the clear yet, and Budli Arnason may have a different opinion about you to me, so you'd better hope that I manage to find out what really happened out there on that track if you want to stay in one piece." With that, he walked back to the hall to tell Aud what he had done. The rest of the housecarls gathered around Hamdir to find out what had gone on, but he stayed silent on the subject and went off to find water and a salve for bruised ribs.

From the hall, a slave was breathlessly rushing towards Grimsson to tell him that a significant visitor had arrived unannounced. Never one to be absent when exciting things were afoot, it was a seeress, the Volva Hrefna. Grimsson sighed. Any Volva should be shown respect and treated well accordingly, and their visits were considered an honour amongst heathen folk. There were, however, several protocols to observe, which he could well do without at a time he was under such pressure to find answers before the Althing met in two days.

Chapter 4

Volva Hrefna certainly knew how to make an impressive entrance. The long hair that framed her wrinkled face may be greying, but her sharp eyes missed nothing as she entered the hall. A mysterious birdskin bag hung from an intricately carved hide belt, which girdled a beautiful blue gown. Her cloak and hood were trimmed with a rare fur, and like many Volvas, she wore catskin mittens. She supported herself with a silver-tipped staff, and there wasn't a man brave enough to touch it without her permission, such was its' magical reputation. It was even rumoured that she kept the shrivelled phallus of a man who had offended her in the bag. No one had actually seen it, but no one was about to ask her about it either. Despite her advanced years, she held herself straight with dignity and authority. "You have a problem" she stated.

"Yes, I have", said Grimsson, eyeing her warily. He ushered her to his own high seat, in respect for her powers and position, and half sat on the corner of a table. She beckoned to Aud to sit beside her, knowing that the couple worked closely together. Good food and drink were rapidly organised for their guest. "The man who died, Erik Snorsson," she resumed "I knew him as a useful servant to Arnason. I helped his mother give birth to him. Arnason will be angry to lose him. He may well turn his anger on you if answers cannot be found."

The Gothi nodded, stroking his beard. "It is a bad business. I am trying hard to get to the bottom of it, but any help would be appreciated. This affair could have repercussions for us all."

"You speak of the clash of our religion with the new one?" his guest checked.

"Yes," he continued. "The murder could be used to discredit people."

"Ah, but which people?" she replied. Grimsson was a little puzzled at this, and it showed on his face. Seeing his discomfort, Aud intervened.

"You have an insight that is different, Volva?"

"Yes, but it is not wholly clear at the moment. I know that reputations are at stake, including your daughter and your man" Grimsson looked up sharply but was reassured. "Do not fret. I see much but say little to most folk."

Grimsson privately thought her powers of observation, coupled with her easy access into most households were as useful as the silver-topped staff and bag of charms. "There is one vision I see but cannot understand. Maybe it will make more sense to you" the Volva continued. "I have seen a dark line in the snow, but do not know what makes it."

'The usual mysterious words that can be interpreted whichever way suits you or the situation' thought Grimsson to himself. He then told the pair that there was a possibility that the rune stave found on the dead man was not the one he originally carried.

Aud exclaimed, "Do you think that the original could still be out there? If it existed, you would think that the murderer would have taken it away with him, although if found on him I suppose it would point to his guilt."

"My very thoughts" echoed Grimsson, gripping the Volva's arm and thanking her profusely. "Maybe the line in the snow is another rune stave?"

"Why don't you go see to your affairs now?" said the Volva, dismissing him. "I have women's business with the Gytha here."

The Gothi was out of the Hof hall before he realised how easily she had taken command of him and reflected ruefully that the Vikings had lost an exceptional potential warrior leader when she was born a woman. Dismissing the thought, he went to find his housecarls, who were practising their sword fighting skills with heavy sticks to avoid unnecessary injury. They regularly practised with a variety of weapons and tactics, including spears, swords, axes and bows. Rolph was drilling them while Grimsson had been otherwise engaged. Grimsson held a hand up to signal a stop and gathered them into a sweating group. "You may need those skills soon," he warned. "You will all be accompanying me to the Althing, and I expect to be in some danger as I present the murder case."

Suddenly the half dozen young men were silent and expectant, in recognition that they may soon have to put their martial skills and courage to the test. "First though I have some other important tasks for you. Atli, I want you to accompany me to the horse fight tomorrow." (There was an audible sigh from several of the men who would have enjoyed the outing, but they knew Atli had lived his early life with a tenant farmer of Hogni.) Grimsson continued "Bragi Hogni will be there with his stallion. You know several of his men. I want you to see what you can find out from them. Particularly, did anyone set out from there through our land just before the time of the murder?"

"I'll do my very best" confirmed Atli, proud of the trust being shown to him.

"The rest of you, I want to return to where the killing happened. Take any spare hands you can round up and do a thorough search around the area. Bring back anything of interest that you find. Particularly look out for a rune stave that may have been discarded. It will probably be about this size," he said, pulling the one from out of his belt bag. "The snow is melting, so it may reveal things that have been hidden up until now. Search thoroughly – a man's life may depend upon it. Be back in time to prepare for the journey to the Althing. All your gear and tents should be in good order already." Rolph confirmed that they were. It was the common practice to arrive the day before the Althing and camp out in booths to be ready for an early start the next morning. Each year the material had to be re-waterproofed with animal fat, and the pairs of hinged carved crossbars of wood, which formed the framework checked for damage and cleaned.

Back in the hall, Aud and the Volva were in deep conversation. Each shared a common faith in the old gods but lived it a different way. Aud assisted her husband in celebrating the seasonal festivals with well-prepared rituals for their small community. The Volva moved from place to place, prophesying and counselling people in a far less rigid way. Each respected the abilities and techniques of the other without wanting to adopt the other's role, although there was some overlap in the methods they used.

After a while, they walked to the women's quarters to join Aud's daughter Gudrun. There they held hands together and sung a long, chanted song, not for the ears of men. Despite an offer of hospitality, the Volva then slipped away quietly, saying she had more work to carry out now that the spring thaw had come.

"Will father and Hamdir be alright?" asked Gudrun anxiously, after the Volva had left.

"Only the Norns know what fate they weave in the lives of men" her mother replied. "Our orlög, the family luck has been good up until now, and they have behaved well before the gods. We have cast our protective magic around our kin and hearth, so now we must let these men carry out the things that they have to do, in their way."

That way involved many tools of metal, all with frighteningly sharp edges. Sven Grimsson was sharpening his sword with a whetstone, thinking darkly to himself what lay ahead with each downward stroke of the stone along the length of the blade.

If either Arnason or Hogni were found guilty of the murder, they were likely to react violently. The local Thing meetings and the national Althing had been started in his father's time to try and resolve disputes. The trouble was that they had no force to ensure that judgements were enforced. If a man had enough warriors on his side, who was to extract the fine or send him away to exile, particularly if his accuser (such as Grimsson) had a much inferior force? The solution often seemed to boil down to having two equal forces keeping a check on each other.

As darkness fell, his men returned empty-handed, having found nothing by the track. "Then go back at first light tomorrow" he ordered, "except for Bjorn and three other men." Bjorn looked startled. "I have a special, secret task for you and three others of your choosing to perform. Come along with me, and I'll tell you about it. I want one of your arrows to" he added. Bjorn followed him dutifully, and next morning was gone with three other friends before even the housecarls had got back to their search. Grimsson still needed to establish some facts, but he couldn't resist the thought that the murder lay with a friend of Bragi Hogni. He would need to keep his wits about him if he were not to lose his own life at the end of this affair, caught between two men of power like a piece on a hnefatafl board. He also needed to protect his family and land, whether he was there to do it or not.

Chapter 5

Despite his master's senior years, Atli had a job to keep pace with him on the walk to the horse fight. Grimsson did not wish to take his one and only own horse to ride, in case anyone should challenge him to compete. He did not want it to be injured as the result of pride or a bet, and as he was not over wealthy, could not easily afford to replace it. Olaf said little on the walk, except to remind Atli to ask questions casually and listen without being noticed. "Do your work while others are busy looking at the horses or me" he instructed.

The place appointed was a natural amphitheatre, formed by an encircling cliff, with a narrow entrance. It was conveniently near a junction of three tracks from East, South and West near Hella. This place was convenient to ensure that the horses were secure, but had the effect of funnelling the North wind, cooled by the nearby glacier to an icy draught which caused men to surreptitiously draw their cloaks closer about them. Of course, being Viking, they would not admit to feeling any hardship but endure it stoically lest it be thought a sign of weakness.

There must have been around a hundred men gathered there, plus a few sellers of food and drink. Grimsson acknowledged the greetings of several men who knew him, without permitting himself to be detained or questioned by them. At one stage he spotted Bragi Hogni across the enclosure and was sure he had turned away from scrutinising him when he realised that he was about to be observed.

The top of an Icelandic horse's head came up to a man's chest, and they were adept at being ridden or pulling a cart in icy conditions. What made them special was their ability to tölt, a very rapid walk, increasing in speed to a canter without shaking the rider about too much. Some also were skilled at skeith or pace.

A mare in season was being led around the smooth area between the rocky surroundings and allowed to urinate there, thus spreading her message of sexual readiness. Then she was led away past her two potential suitors, giving a coquettish whinny as she was taken away. They strained at their halters and were then paraded for all to see. Bets were placed and opinions offered amongst the crowd. One stallion was owned by Hogni, who was a keen competitor in such contests, but he stood proudly by whilst his minions both restrained and goaded the horse.

Its mane had been trimmed back short revealing a black stripe cutting through the dun colour. The second horse was off-white, slightly shorter but with powerful hindquarters. A tenant farmer called Ljot, who was trying to improve his status, had devoted his winter to training it and stood by confidently with a long goad in his hand.

Meanwhile, Atli had left his master's side, and was greeting old friends from Bragi's camp. He soon engaged them in talk about their horses. Subtly, he enquired how things were going at their farmstead. "Excellent" was the reply. "He is a hard master but determined to get on and succeed. He is trying to establish himself as a merchant, and has put money into building a new ship, ready to sail as soon as the gales die away."

"Wouldn't fancy living there though" Atli teased "a bit far from the centre of things to see much of the world."

"Those who want to travel can always go on voyages with him or even his son Harald Hognisson. Last year Harald went to the court of Olaf Tryggvason in Norway. He came back bearing marvellous gifts from him and the holy men who are there."

"And a lot of them new Christian ideas" added his colleague sourly.

"You wouldn't know one god from another!" was his friend's swift riposte, "Unless they have taken to living in mead horns," he added, laughing. The other grinned in sheepish agreement.

Turning back to Atli, he added indignantly "We have our share of visitors."

"Sorry, I did not mean offence."

"We get plenty of people trying to sell him stuff. They know he needs materials for his future voyages."

"What even recently, during the bad weather?"

"Not so many then – just a seller of spear and axe heads."

"Is he still there?" ventured Atli.

"No, he left a week ago."

Atli could hardly contain his excitement but tried to feign disinterest. "Oh, those fellows are all the same – the goods are never as good as the samples they show. Was it that old rogue Skrall?"

"No, an Orkneyinger called Skrimsson" was the reply.

"He didn't call at our place" continued Atli, hoping to find out where the merchant went.

"Too small!" the other man teased eager to get in a jibe back. "I think he had bigger fish to catch over at Hasmingen." Atli smothered a smile. He recognised the name as the home of Arnason at Selfoss.

Just then the long-awaited equine clash was finally brought about, and in the excitement, Atli managed to slip back to the Gothi.

"You look as though you have found something out," the older man said, seeing the smile on the face of Atli, who nodded enthusiastically. "Keep it until the journey home" he growled from the corner of his mouth, turning this to a toothy smile for a rather nosy neighbour who was approaching him, no doubt to gather gossip.

Nostrils flared, ears went back, and warning snorts and wild eyes confronted each other as the two horses were released to face each other. Veins swelled visibly, and they were soon up on their hindquarters, for the entire world like two vicious men in a fistfight. Flashes of hard hooves scythed through the midday air as the crowd encouraged their favourites on. Their heads and necks twisted, each seeking an opening or advantage over the other. Suddenly, Bragi's horse made a particularly aggressive pawing lunge against the flank of its rival, using its superior height. The other horse failed to turn away quickly enough. His hide ran red with blood, and men ran forward to separate them, but the victor chased the defeated stallion with bared, biting teeth to its retreating rump, despite vicious rear hooves kicking back in defence. Finally, the men managed to hang onto trailing ropes and restrained the beasts. Bragi raised a hand in salute to the crowd with the broad smile of a man assured he is still a winner. Those who had predicted the outcome correctly cheered and sought out others who owed them wagers.

Atli was disappointed to be dragged away so quickly, but as his master said, men wagering, often with the help of a drink was not an activity to encourage polite, social conversation. He waited until they were clear of the press of excited men before asking Atli to tell his tale and did not spare praise for the man finding out so much. "Knowledge can be sharper than a sword" he counselled. Atli wasn't altogether sure of the significance of what he had been found out but walked home in the glow of his master's encouragement and the promise of a whole drinking horn of best mead to himself. While the mead would be a welcome treat, it would also be a mark of status with his comrades. He was aware of being regarded as the right-hand man of his friend Rolph, rather than as a man in his own right. Grimsson was not unaware of this either but chose to allow men to rise or fall by their merits and endeavours, rather than by intervening on their behalf. He did try, however, to encourage each man to do his best and take pride in himself. Warriors who were self-confident were far more effective and motivated to defend their master and home.

Atli told Grimsson something else he had picked up, which he found incredible. "Apparently, the Christians aren't allowed to eat horse meat. What an earth would they do with a dead horse?" he wondered.

"And how will some of the poorer ones survive the winter?" replied the Gothi, shaking his head in disbelief. "Although last year, a Christian man called Kjartan subjected himself to a dry fast during their Lent festival. He restricted himself to fish, whale, bread, vegetables, nuts and fruit."

"No meat for a month!" exclaimed Atli incredulously.

"Oh yes, some people visited him from far away to see the wonder" added Grimsson, recalling the story from a friend at the Althing last year.

It was late afternoon by the time they got back to the farmstead but could see that the search party had beaten them. "I hope this means that they have found something worthwhile" Olaf muttered as he quickened his pace. From the look on Giuki's face as he reached the yard, he knew they had.

Having searched in ever-increasing circles from the still bloodstained patch of snow, it had been Giuki who had painfully grasped the flat wooden object from a thorny bush into which it had been thrown. "Not a dark line in the snow, it seems, but valuable object none the less" exclaimed Grimsson to his wife as he sat to examine it. It was common pinewood, and he traced a finger over its scratched incisions. 'Bragi, Yes you can sail with me, friend. Be ready soon after the Althing. Arnason' he had read aloud.

"There is no hate there," exclaimed Aud.

"No, simply an arrangement to sail together on a trading voyage. There is always a greater safety against pirates that way." He also enlightened her regarding Atli's information. "So, the spear head seller could have taken a message to Arnason then, possibly before Snorsson set back with a reply," he thought aloud.

Aud added, "The message is obviously a reply to one from Bragi – it starts with the word yes." Her husband nodded his agreement.

"Why wouldn't the spear seller bring a reply back?" his wife asked, after thinking a while.

"Probably going onto somewhere else I suppose. Although it is early in the year for such journeying, I suppose whoever arrives first at a settlement has the better chance of a sale. Yet, he could see everyone who was coming to the Althing just by setting up a stall with the others outside. He could certainly rely on seeing both

Hogni and Arnason, as they are always known to attend." His voice trailed off in thought.

Later, he carved a message of his own on a piece of wood. Summoning a trusted servant called Arlaf, he told him to set off the next morning to deliver it to Arnason. "You may bring a reply, plus anything he may give you directly to me at the Althing. It is pointless for you to come back here first."

Chapter 6

That night in the Hof hall, Grimsson raised a horn of mead to his men, having rewarded Giuki as well as Atli with their portions. Aud took the communal horn from man to man, as was her right and duty as the head of the household, and toasts were drunk. Later, she led the women from the hall to their quarters, leaving the men to conduct their Blot ritual.

They stripped off their shirts and built up a throbbing rhythm by clapping, stamping and hoarse yells. The Gothi brought forward a bowl of blood from a slaughtered goat, and frequently dipping a branch into the bowl, sprinkled each man's head or chest until they were all bespattered. At a signal, they all stopped together, and there was a startling, pregnant silence. After a suitably dramatic pause, the Gothi gave a traditional greeting, to all men present, the ancestors, the spirit Wight's of the land and the Vanir and Aesir gods and goddesses. Then he led them in a chanting of the twenty-four rune sounds, each of which has a depth of magical meaning and worth, in addition to their properties for writing. The air was pungent with the peat smoke, sweaty bodies and the smell of the roasting goat carcass.

It was usual for there to be invocations to Odin, Thor & Frey, but tonight Grimsson added one to Tyr. The older men nodded wisely, knowing the tale of how Tyr had made a sacrifice of his hand to Fenris wolf to save the other Gods from his ever-widening jaws. Several men caught the symbolism and quietly explained it to those around them, while the cooked goat was passed around on a wooden platter as a Sumbel sacred feast, with the men snatching hot pieces in their hands, since no knives were allowed in the sacredly created Ve ritual space.

Then a substantial ceremonial drinking horn was filled with mead and blessed by Grimsson making the sign of a Thorshammer over it. It was passed from man to man and each drunk a toast of his choosing. It may be to his specific patron God or Goddess, or for more general things such as success at fishing, or the year's harvest. It was noticeable how many chose to wish good luck to the Gothi at the Althing in two days' time, and it was clear that there was a general understanding as to what was going on.

The horn circulated again, and this was a chance for men to make personal oaths. Grimsson took off his arm ring and dipped it in a bowl of the blood from the goat. Each oath maker gripped this in turn as they declaimed their words. While there was the usual selection of promises to work harder for personal ambitions, much comment was passed upon the oath made by Hamdir, on maintaining his loyalty and defending with all his might his master, Grimsson. The rest of the housecarls joined in, to a man, but Olaf was pleased to see how Hamdir had taken the lead and had born him no apparent ill will for the blow and the words he had delivered the other day.

Finally, a young man who was skilled at the bird bone flute was persuaded to play. One of the older men, a noted skald poet who emphasised and illustrated his story by plucking and strumming a lyre recounted a favourite tale of how Thor lost and regained his hammer. It was one considered unsuitable for when women were present, and so the men had a raucous, bawdy laugh together at the humour woven into the myth by the storyteller. As their host rose to go to bed, so did they, albeit reluctantly. Even those who were not travelling to the Althing the next day had preparations to make for those who were.

Soon after, Aud rejoined her husband in bed. She was fearful of what tomorrow would bring yet unwilling to add to his worries. Grimsson was aware though and took her in his great muscular arms. "I will speak the truth at the Althing" he stated simply.

"I would not expect you to do anything else, but it will not be pleasant for some folk to hear" replied Aud, biting her lip and trying desperately to keep a calm voice.

"You must stay here and ensure our home is kept safe" he instructed. "Just in case, get the thralls to fill as many containers with water as possible. Some would think nothing of trying to burn us out of our hall" he spat. "You know where our small treasure is hidden, in the chest I brought back from the Saxons?"

"Of course, dear" Aud replied, "but it will not come to that will it?" She knew that he was indicating her course of action should he not return. 'Damn bravery and honour' she thought to herself. 'That her good man may suffer death through behaving correctly.' Then she checked herself for unworthy thoughts. He had no choice, and as his wife and Gytha, neither did she.

"I hope it will not" he replied, interrupting her thoughts with an answer. "But it would be foolish not to be prepared. Your old bear has a bit of a plan" he chuckled, pointing to his head with his finger and winking in a way he hoped was reassuring.

She knew that he could be wily as well as brave, but the gesture only partly comforted her. Aud could not reply, so hugged him harder. With the familiarity, which comes with a long marriage, they caressed each other slowly and lovingly, and fell together for love, for desperation and reassurance that there was some good left in their world. The release they felt was urgent and complete, and in the knowledge that this may be the last time they enjoy it. Savouring the close feeling, Aud fell asleep with her head on Sven's chest, which was still streaked with the blood of the Blot, and the sweat of his recent exertions.

Grimsson rose early the next morning and walked just wrapped in his cloak to the hot spring pool that was his private bathing place. The mineral-tinged water warmed by volcanic activity far below bubbled through a fissure just above a natural rocky basin. It flowed down into it via a channel he had scraped away. Stepping gingerly down the flat stones he had placed as steps, he eased himself in with a sigh, enjoying the warm sensation. After a satisfying soak and a rub around his body with some leaves that produced a light foam, he reluctantly got out, wrapping his now wet body back in the cloak, and rubbing himself dry. He returned to the hall on the wooden walkway that had been built on his instructions to avoid mud and sharp stones on clean bare feet.

Back in his chamber, the thrall woman who did the laundry had laid out his best shirt, tunic and trousers on the bed. After he had dressed and put on his armring and Thorshammer pendant, his wife came up behind him and kneeling on the bed started to comb his hair and beard with a finely crafted antler comb. Of course, he was capable of doing this himself, but this was a loving act from a woman wanting to say so much but not daring to start. It had all been said before when he had set off on warlike voyages with his comrades in the past. As she combed, she remembered the handsome, athletic youth she had married, and smiled secretly at the signs of age that were beating him in a way no enemy ever had. The greying and thinning of the hair, the slight thickening of the waist ate away at the image of youthful vigour. She paused to untangle a strand of his beard and could see why this intimate act performed by another woman was thought of in their laws as grounds for divorce in the same way as lying with a man was. Finally, when he felt that he had been fussed over quite enough, he rose from the edge of the bed, and they went together to eat.

There was nobody to dress the hair of Hamdir Gettirsson, as he stood erect in clean clothes, with beard and nails clipped in the corner of the hall, where he had his straw mattress laid on an upturned bench. He was determined to do his best in service to the Gothi, including defending him with his own life if necessary. He had assumed that attitude, along with his training, but it didn't stop the fear that whispered in his ear. Instinctively, his hand went to his throat, touching the Thorshammer that hung there for courage.

His ear alerted by the whisper of his name from the doorway. Leaving his comrades still waking up he crossed cautiously to see who was summoning him from behind the door, which was just ajar. Hidden from the occupants of the hall around the great wooden structure was Gudrun with a bundle in her arms. She thrust it out at him, hardly daring to speak. It was a new brown tunic she had made. He held it up to the light admiring it. "It is a fine tunic, which I would gladly accept as a gift from you, but I don't want to get you into trouble with your father," he said uncertainly.

"Damn my father," she said vehemently. "He puts you all into danger. I wish it were a mail shirt I had made to protect you, instead of this, but I am not an armourer. My wishes have gone into every stitch, though. Wear it for me" She flushed at her own boldness.

"I love you," he said "but I also honour and respect your father. He has been very good to me, and I do not want to break his trust. I need to gain his acceptance of me so that we can be together properly." He hadn't quite meant for the words to rush out this way. He realised that what he had just said almost constituted a proposal and was unsure what to do as the morning light played on the upturned face of Gudrun, who was looking at him with undisguised admiration.

Hamdir stepped forward and stroked her flushed cheek with his finger. Finding no resistance, he leaned forward to kiss her. She responded with passion, but aware of the stirrings of others within the hall. They reluctantly broke away from each other. "Go safely at the Althing" she urged.

"I will be surrounded in our love" was the reply.

Later, less courage was being shown in the women's quarters by Gudrun Svensdottir. She lay coiled into a ball, quietly sobbing to herself, in the knowledge that she may never see Hamdir alive again after today. Her hands twisted her hair, and she felt as lonely as the far mountains, and as powerless as the fish on a baited line to influence what would happen next.

Over on the coast, Bjorn and his three handpicked companions were leaving his mother's fish curing shed, carrying a boat that had been stored for the winter. They grunted and heaved it to the sea, carrying it upturned on their aching shoulders. They sweated, despite the chill of the morning air blowing in from the sea. At the shore's edge, they turned it upright, and launched it into the breaking waves, scrambling aboard and grabbing oars. They pulled westwards towards the mouth of the River Thjorsa and struggled hard to beach it again amongst the torrential flow of water from the melting snows upstream meeting the sea. Having beached the vessel, there was no hope of rowing it upstream against that flow. Once again, they shouldered the inverted craft, and using the butt ends of the oars to aid them, started the slow ascent up the wild track that ran alongside the riverbank. It was an unsteady, tiring trek, but with frequent stops, they carried on up the hill. It was to be whole day's expedition, sometimes requiring them to haul with ropes to raise it through the narrower sections of the incline. When they were close to the edge of the plain where the river ran over a cliff in an elementally powerful waterfall, they stopped. Inverting the boat on some rocks made a crude shelter to sleep for the night. The dried fish and bread from Bjorn's mother were washed down with water that flowed past them at a dizzying, mesmerising speed. Their talk before falling asleep from their exertions centred around why the Gothi wanted them to do this, and would it be safe to launch the boat into such a swift-flowing river?

Chapter 7

There were aquamarine coloured pools of water, reflecting the bright spring sky over Thingvellir Plain, yet some still had shards of ice glistening in the sunshine. Overlooking the plain was a formidable chain of flat-topped mountains. Their frozen white skins were delineated with blue-grey veins of rock protruding through, which some said were the bones of the primaeval giant Ymir. In contrast to the enormity of the landscape, the men who milled about with their tents and animals, carts and belongings, thoughts and fears, appeared insignificantly small. Yet this was the focus of all who were there, not the grandeur of what to them were familiar surroundings. The roar of Oxarafoss, the nearby waterfall on the Axe River that raced past the site of their deliberations, mocked the futility of humans trying to decide their destiny amidst the elemental forces that surrounded them.

Grimsson's booth had already been erected as he had instructed by two servants who went ahead with an ox cart. It had been set up to the rear of the flat camping ground on Thingvellir plain, with its back to the Axe river in a gap between some rocks and bushes. Most men strove to get their tented booths in the front rank, close to the meeting and as a visible sign of their attendance. Grimsson himself arrived on his horse, escorted on foot by his half dozen housecarls. He waved a greeting to some acquaintances as he passed but took care not to become involved in any lengthy conversations. He was not in the mood for politics and factionalism that often proceeded the next day's council. He chose Sigurd and Sorli to take the first sentry duty outside the booth and said for the others to amuse themselves around the site, as long as they did not get involved in any disputes or brawls. "I would also like you to find out some information," he said and detailed what he was after. To Rolph, he set an extra task, giving him a newly made rune stave to take with him. Coincidentally just after this, his servant Arlaf delivered one to him from Arnason, having accompanied the man and his party to the Althing.

Later, there was a disturbance outside the booth, and as he stood up to investigate a large heavily armoured man burst in, sending the sentries flying. He was tall and well- built and carried the weight of his chainmail suit without any discomfort. Raising his hand to signal the sentries not to counter-attack yet, Grimsson asked, "What is it?"

"A warning! Don't get involved with the affairs of those of superior position and force to you. If you do, you'll regret it!" The bloodshot eyes and flushed appearance indicated he had probably been drinking since his arrival, but he still appeared a formidable threat.

Before Grimsson could make a reply or reach for a weapon, the tent darkened as the tent flap was almost blotted out by a man even larger than the first, who shouted "You!" with a fierce, vehement yell at the back of the intruder's head. As the man turned a head butt hit him full in the face from a skull encased in a battered metal helmet. The intruder fell instantly, blood pouring from his nose and a bruised eye already closing. "Hmm – I never liked Karl. He should have better manners than to enter without invitation and insult my friend" the rescuer snarled.

"I wonder who he was from" mused Grimsson.

"I doubt we'll find out" laughed the attacker as the two embarrassed sentries dragged the unconscious man away by his feet. The new visitor had a ruddy face, marked with a scar across one cheek, and overgrown eyebrows that threatened to dangle in his twinkling eyes. He had a broad, rascally grin on his lips and a cloak of brown fur around his shoulders and back. The two old comrades fell together in a bear-like hug.

"Grettir Onundarson" exclaimed Grimsson. "Trouble attracts you like a fish to salt, but thanks for your help."

"My old friend Sven" was the return greeting. "How's that boy of mine Hamdir?"

"Not a boy for a long time. Sit down, and I'll tell you about him." Grettir sat on his cloak, which he folded beneath him and accepted some mead while he heard of his son's recent exploits and their conclusion.

"You treated him lightly, but I guess he is his father's son" was his comment at the end, with an air of thinly-disguised pride. "He sounds to have grown into a good, honourable man under your tutelage, as I expected. But what is he like as a warrior? Which weapons does he favour?" asked his father, who had himself raised belligerence to an art form.

The two men talked at some length about Hamdir, his prowess at poetry as well as at arms and his future. They were still talking when the rest of the housecarls returned in high spirits. Hamdir greeted his father warmly and exchanged news. Some of the housecarls had made some small purchases from the traders, whilst others had witnessed a wrestling match between two massive fishermen up from the coast. Rolph sidled quietly up to Grimsson during their spirited description of this and handed him back the rune stave. "It is as you thought, Gothi," he said simply. Grimsson winked and thanked him and pocketed the stave into his pouch.

The others had also seen both Arnason and Hogni about with a full complement of retainers. Some food was produced, and some of the earlier tension was dispensed as they chewed on flatbread and sausages made from lard, blood and meat. Afterwards, Sorli urged their visitor to tell of some of his battle exploits. In deference to his host, he chose to describe the raid they had both taken part in on Gippeswic and Maeldune. He talked of the mighty shield wall, never broken with each man behind it a deadly force to be reckoned with. They laughed at the naivety of Brythnoth the Saxon Ealdorman, in allowing the Vikings off the island causeway where they were at a disadvantage, to the main shore where their superior number, weaponry and experience overwhelmed the Saxons. "The Danegeld we extracted after that was some of the heaviest booty we had ever seen. There is many a man who set himself up with land and animals from that time" explained Onundarson, "Although of course some were less lucky and only got a warriors death for their efforts." There was a realisation there for some of the younger men that glory did not always lead to a more comfortable life here in the Midgard Earth, and the mood was more subdued as darkness fell.

Eventually, the younger men went to sleep in their booth next door to Grimsson, leaving two sentries to guard Sven Grimsson and Grettir Onundarson who continued talking with each other. Sven opened his heart to his old friend, whom he knew he could trust. Finally, the other said, "You know I am no good at law speaking. I haven't the head for it. I've been grateful for the way you've brought up my son as your own while I was away on voyages. He was too young to take with me, and there is no place for a berserker anymore. We are a dying breed; thought of as bullies rather than the noble warrior cult we once aspired to. These new ideas catching on are likely to degrade us further, and I've no mind to miss out on the warrior's home Valhalla through straw death in bed or sea death out on another voyage. So, I'm throwing in my lot with you if you'll have me. There'll be plenty more like Karl in the coming days if I'm not mistaken." It was the longest speech that his friend had ever heard him make, and he grasped his arm and said "I would be honoured to have you with me, though we may both face Valhalla in the next few days. Only the Norns of fate know the answer to that, but at least we'll take a few with us, eh?" He then went on to explain his plans, after which they both tried to get some sleep until morning.

Chapter 8

The light from the tent flap dazzled Grimsson as he woke to the sound of his servants bringing food, drink and a bowl of water to freshen his face and hands. Grettir Onundarson soon woke also and joined him. When they had finished one of the servants named Bryth was addressed by his master, who handed him a single war arrow with his runic signature on it. "Keep this safe and hidden. If there is trouble later today, you must take my horse and ride away as fast as you can to my two tenant farmer bondsmen. Show them the arrow as a token that they must send all available armed men to my farm without any delay. Then go there yourself and warn my wife Aud what has happened. Ride fast and wear my cloak with the hood up. You may well be pursued if they think it is I on the horse, but they will not catch you if you get a good start. Understood?" The man affirmed that he had. He was not much use as a warrior, but as a horseman, he was superb and had often found excuses to ride his master's horse in the past. "You must not go unless it gets worse" reiterated Grimsson. "I don't want folk to think I'm starting a war."

Before they left the booth, Grimsson touched his Thorshammer and asked the Gods for strength and wisdom. In the old days there had been communal worship before the Althing, but with religion now a divisive force, it was considered less offensive for each man to follow his beliefs privately. His men murmured their thoughts to, and then by mutual consent, all strode together to the gathering. A grave-looking individual stepped forward and touched Grimsson's sleeve. It was the leader of the Althing, Thorgeir Thorkelson from Ljosavatn Farm, near the Lightwater Lake. He had obtained his unenviable position solely through election as the largest landholder and looked splendid in a wolfskin cloak, great gold neck torc and high sealskin boots. Although he had a florid, plump face and figure, he was known as a fair-minded man, who tried to stay neutral in all things. He was about the same age as Grimsson, and they had known each other as younger men. "You still intend to present the case of the killing?" he asked.

"Yes, it is my duty" was the reply.

"I am concerned for your safety" the leader stated quietly.

"So am I but feel I must proceed. When judgement is considered and delivered, will I have fulfilled my duty?" asked Grimsson, feigning an innocent, unconcerned look.

"Of course," replied Thorgeir, with a glimmer of a smile. "You have urgent business no doubt to attend to when you have finished speaking the law I expect. The accused will have to stay until a decision is taken on guilt and damages." The man looked directly into his old friend's face as he said this, to ensure the underlying message was communicated. "There are two short cases before yours – a divorce and simple theft," he added. It was his prerogative as to the order of cases, and he had clearly decided to get this one sorted out early in the week of hearings to avoid factions or alliances building up and complicating the situation further.

"Thank you for your enlightenment" was the Gothi's ironic reply, following him into the area where the Althing was almost assembled. Anyone who wished to could attend during the two weeks that the Althing lasted, but only the thirty-six Gothi could vote. It was crowded with many men. All had left their weapons in their booths since they were forbidden here. "Keep every one of our men together near the edge of the crowd" whispered Grimsson to Rolph as proceedings started.

A woman requested a divorce since her husband had beaten her and taken a slave into their bed. He did not turn up to contest it, so judgement was easily in her favour. An order was made that her brothers could recover the morning gift and bride price from him on her behalf. The bride price paid by her parents as a dowry was not large but would enable her to re-establish herself. The morning gift was hers by right, having been given by her husband on the morning after their wedding night, in lieu of taking her honour.

The thief had been caught in the act, stealing a side of ham hanging in a barn by the owner. The thief bore signs of rough treatment and did not say much when he was stripped of his citizenship and made a slave to whoever would bid for him. The small slave price went to the owner of the ham. Few were willing to take the thief as a slave as he had lost his previous employment through being lazy. He had tried to steal the bacon to try and survive. There were a few sneering comments about how he may have been able to beg for bread but was unlikely to taste such undeserved good food again.

Finally, Thorgeir Thorkelson announced the case for the killing of Erik Snorsson. The crowd went quiet, and it was evident that rumours had spread and that this was the focus of interest for the day. At a nod from Thorgeir, Grimsson stepped forward and stood upon the slightly elevated law rock, which was also used by Thorgeir to recite a portion of the law later in the week. Grimsson cleared his throat and began.

"Erik Snorsson was found dead on my land. Our laws state that I must investigate the cause, which I have done to the best of my ability. My servant Bjorn, who was returning from a trip to his mother's on the coast, found him. He did not know the man and has a good character, so I have no reason to suspect him, especially as a coin was still in the man's purse, suggesting robbery for money was not the motive. He came straight to my farm and told me what he had found. My men went and fetched the body. There was a wound to the chest, and his knife was still in its sheath." Turning, he asked "Budli Arnason, do you know any reason why he may have been killed?"

"No, I don't" was the fierce reply. "He was a good man with no enemies as far as I know. I have lost a good and trusted servant."

"Good enough for you to entrust him with a message?" interrupted Grimsson.

"Yes, but what has that got to do with it?" came the response.

"Almost everything," said Grimsson mysteriously. "Can you confirm that he was taking a message when he was killed?"

"Yes, I can" confirmed Arnason. "It was to Bragi Hogni."

"Was it a reply to a message he sent you?"

"It was," said Arnason tersely. He was a cautious man as a rule and did not like his business aired in public.

"I sent a message to you the other day, asking you to let me see that first message, which you have. I will read it aloud now if that is alright?" Arnason nodded grimly.

"Budli: Can I sail with you to Norway? – Bragi. You sent him a reply?" Grimsson asked, already knowing the answer.

"I did" snapped Arnason, unused to being questioned by anyone.

"This is the rune stave I took from the pouch of the dead man" continued Grimsson, holding it up. "It says Bragi: Kill Grimsson before the Althing. He is the main obstacle – Budli."

There was a gasp around the crowd of men, and Grimsson saw in the face of Budli Arnason no lesser astonishment. "I never wrote that!" he shouted indignantly. "It is a trick or a lie. You are trying to discredit me here, Grimsson" he continued." Men started looking at each other and started arguing between themselves.

"Admit it" chipped in Bragi Hogni, directing his remarks to Arnason. "You want him out of the way for his land and our religion. I only wanted to sail with you for mutual protection, not to be your hired assassin!"

Thorgeir Thorkelsson, the head of the Althing stepped forward and appealed for calm. "No truth will be found while men hurl insults at each other" he counselled. The tumult decreased to a few loud whispers. Taking the opportunity, Grimsson continued in a conciliatory tone. "You are right to be aggrieved at someone trying to discredit you, Arnason. I, for one, believe you did no such thing, and that someone else is trying to discredit you." After a pause for dramatic effect, he turned, and pointing said: "Namely, Bragi Hogni!"

"How dare you?" sneered Hogni. "Trying to divert the blame for a death on your land by accusing me. I suppose you had a vision from the runes, you old heathen" he spat sarcastically.

"Well it is true the rune stave talked to me" smiled Grimsson, "but not in the way you might expect. It told me you carved it." With that Hogni lunged forward, intent on doing some physical damage to his inquisitor, but he was caught and restrained by men near him. "Let the Gothi speak," said one, "either to condemn himself or to show the truth." It was a bad moment, and Grimsson took a deep breath before continuing. "Could any men skilled with wood step forward?" he asked. Four shuffled forward curiously. He handed the stave to them and asked, "What do you make of the wood?" They didn't take long to confer amongst themselves and come up with an answer. "It is the special red oak wood from Vinland. Only Bragi Hogni has it here in Iceland." A low murmur ran around the assembly.

"Anyone could have taken that scrap" protested Hogni. "It is obviously an offcut."

"I agree," said Grimsson disarmingly, "but how would you explain the matching edges with this other one?" With that, he produced the stave that Arnason had delivered, and brought the two together for all to see over his head. It was apparent they were two adjacent pieces from the same section of red oak. There were audible gasps and a lot of excitable talk.

"Just because it is my wood, doesn't mean that I carved it" defended Hogni.

"Then who else on your land can carve runes?" asked his accuser, already knowing the answer. "I understand your son Harald Hognisson uses the new Christian writing." There was some muffled laughter from some at this. It was well known that the son had argued with his father on the matter and refused to use anything, but the Latin alphabet associated with his new religion. Referring to this, Grimsson taunted "Isn't it true that you can only write in runes, and your son only the new writing?"

"I shall be learning the new writing to" Hogni, attempting to hide a scowl and regain his composure. "But I shall still need to write runes for others who do not know it."

"That is understandable" came back Grimsson, "But isn't it true that nobody else knows how to write in either way at your settlement?"

"Nobody to my knowledge" Hogni admitted reluctantly. "They have no need."

"Then I must deduce that you wrote the runes on the piece of wood that could only have come from your yard" reiterated Grimsson to make sure the assembly had registered the point as a logical, unemotional argument.

"But I could not have murdered the man" countered Hogni. "I have been at my farm these last few weeks. Everyone will confirm that."

There were nods and growls of consent from his men.

"Indeed, I believe you," said Grimsson. "I believe the rune stave was swapped by an Orkneyinger called Skrimsson, who also committed the murder. He is outside at his stall. I would like him brought before the Althing." Several men immediately volunteered, and the bewildered and frightened spear seller was roughly bundled into the midst of the crowd, who parted away from him as if to avoid physical contact or guilt by association.

Before Grimsson could re-commence his questioning, Hogni who had been given a chance to think in the pause in proceedings seized his opportunity with an accusation. "I gave him a message to take to Arnason concerning joining forces for a voyage – you have already seen it, found by Grimsson's men. Skrimsson must have done the switch on the answer. He must know how to carve runes."

The subject of the attack shook his head in disbelief and denial. Intervening, the Gothi appeared to take his part. "I know you cannot read runes. Yesterday I carved my own stave and sent it to him by one of my men. It said, "Could you supply twenty spears, and for how much silver?" He told my man he could not read it. My man did not know the meaning either. I think any merchant would have read the runes for such an order." There was a general whisper of agreement. Skrimsson also clearly stated that this was true and that he did not know it was one of Grimsson's men delivering the message.

"Fair enough. I think we all accept that you cannot read or write runes" continued Grimsson. No one protested, so he continued "But you will admit to delivering a message to Arnason from Hogni?"

The man saw no reason to deny this – it was well known to others. "Yes, I was travelling to Hasmingen, the hall of Arnason to sell my wares, so it was no trouble to deliver the rune stave at the same time. I do not know what it said," he added.

"At Arnason's, you left quite quickly, and said you were going to continue your journey and try to sell some axe and spearheads?"

"Yes, I need the trade" was the eager reply.

"So, it would make sense for you to continue towards the West. It would make no sense to double back to places you had already passed, such as my farmstead would it?" led on the Gothi.

"Oh no." the spear seller agreed, unsure of where this was all leading.

"So where did you go to then?" The tone of Grimsson hardened as he sprung his trap with this very direct question. The man looked around nervously, and a panicky look came to his face. His hands grasped at air, and a sweat broke on his forehead. Breaking down he pointed to Bragi Hogni. "You said you would protect me, look after me!" he accused. The crowd gathered their conclusions from this outburst as Hogni glowered furiously.

Grimsson turned to address the crowd. "Did any of you receive him at your halls after his visit to Arnason?" The question was almost rhetorical, and nobody spoke. "As I thought" he continued. "Because I believe that he followed after Erik Snorsson and caught up with him on my land. Snorsson would not suspect any treachery from someone he had seen at Arnason's hall, so it would have been easy for Skrimsson to approach close and stab him. Then he could swap over the second rune stave supplied by Hogni. He then threw away the original stave into a bush, not wanting it to be found on him. It was that stave that my man found later in the thorn bush, revealed by the melted snow.

Skrimsson looked terrified. He knew that the game was up, and from the accusing looks and murmur directed towards him, he had no possibility of escape. He didn't see why he should shoulder the blame alone. Pointing at Hogni, he trembled, but shouted, "It was him that got me to do it. With Arnason discredited he could take over the main trading trips to Norway and Denmark, and his son could be made a bishop. Together they would have great power and influence, and his main rival Arnason would be unable to compete against him."

Arnason, who had stayed relatively calm until now stepped forward, with a thunderous countenance. Addressing Hogni, he rasped "I thought you were my friend, both of us Christians together. Is this the shameful way you treat me? You stayed safe in your hall, getting this wretch to do your dirty work. You disgust me!"

"It is all that old heathen's fault" replied Hogni. "Dividing us against ourselves. It is time this Althing committed itself to the true religion." Several arguments were breaking out amongst the crowd now until Thorgeir shouted "Enough!" in a commanding voice that alerted his unarmed yet numerous pugnacious retainers to ensure that his wishes were met. The row subsided. Impressing his authority, he continued. "This discussion is not about religion. That is for another day. I think we have all heard enough, haven't we?" His gaze around the crowd defied any man to say otherwise. "Say if you believe that Hogni sent Skrimsson to kill the messenger and swap rune staves." Some bolder or more impetuous men shouted affirmation straight away, while others looked around first to see how others had voted. Some feared revenge if Hogni was found not to be guilty, but seeing the way it was going, and aware of the possibility of Arnason seeking revenge for anyone not voting as he felt, they also complied.

"We have a clear decision" continued Thorgeir. "I congratulate Grimsson on his presentation of the case. You are now free to step away to your business," he added with a slight bow of dismissal. As Grimsson swiftly left with his men, Thorgeir started organising a group of three elders to consider penalties and compensation. Their eventual decision took some time and was not announced until long after Grimsson had departed. It involved a year's exile for Hogni, and two small farms as compensation to Arnason and Grimsson. Hogni was to be quit of Iceland within three days, or his life would be forfeit. Skrimsson was made a slave.

Some of Hogni's men watched Grimsson, and his party while the elders were consulting. They saw them hurriedly all squeeze into their two booths. They thought that while they were inside there, they could await their master's instructions, which would probably be to attack them on their way home, maybe by overtaking them with the string of horses Hogni owned. They waited in vain for Grimsson to re-emerge, but he and his men had left immediately by cutting the fabric at the back of the booths and making their escape between the bushes and rocks against which the booths had been erected on Grimsson's instructions.

Then the fooled men were tricked once more as they spotted a man in Grimsson's cloak astride his horse leaving the Althing. There was confusion as they ran about trying to catch an available horse and saddle it to pursue him. By the time they had left, he was far away. Nobody found out the true identity and purpose of Bryth until long afterwards after he had delivered the war arrow to the bondsmen farmers. With Grimsson apparently left those bent on revenge crossed to the booths of Grimsson, and finally discovered his escape. They set off in pursuit.

Chapter 9

Grimsson and his housecarls, two of his servants and Grettir Onundarson ran at a steady trot towards the ford over the Axe River. Then they skirted north of the Thingvallavatn Lake until they hit the main road for Hella for a short distance. Grimsson planned not to stay on this track for too long. Although it was the obvious and most direct route back to his farm, it had several narrow defiles where he may be ambushed, and additionally might get caught by pursuers on horseback. He knew Hogni and Arnason both had plenty of horses. It was for that reason he had planned to get away on a route impassable to horses. Turning off the main track where the Thjorsa River crossed beneath a bridge and tumbled over a cliff in a waterfall, he and his party followed the river's steep eastern path. The river flowed over the ridge in a startling white wall of frothing liquid, swollen by the melting ice of the mountains across the plain.

It went against their principles to retreat in any way, but they reluctantly admitted they were massively outnumbered by the force of Bragi they had left behind them at the Althing. Nevertheless, each was armed and armoured now. The young men all had the helmets with eye protection as well as nose guards, while Grimsson and Onundarson preferred the older style, with reinforced ornamented eyebrows. The protection was less, but both felt they had far better sideways vision, and in any case, the nose guards blocked most blows to the face. Both of the older men had mail shirts over a padded jacket, but these were expensive items to buy, so the housecarls had to rely on hard leather jerkins to give some protection to the body. Grimsson's mail shirt was a little tight. He had taken it off a Saxon he had killed, so it never fitted that well, but his increasing girth made it a little tighter still to move in. They had brought spears, swords, battle axe and bows as well as their round shields, individually decorated to each man's preference. Some had an additional coat of leather covering the beechwood beneath, and all had a central round domed boss of metal, guarding the handgrip behind it.

As they scrambled down the steep gully, frequently splashed by icy drops of water from the torrent on their right they could see Bjorn and his three companions are stirring themselves beside the fishing boat. It was alongside the river near to an overhanging rock. "It will be hard to launch and guide the boat in this torrent" panted Sigurd, eying the foam and debris hurtling seawards.

"The tears of the mountain giantess weeping stop for no man" laughed Atli, showing off the fact that he had at least memorised one old poem. The sharp-eyed Giuki pointed to the horizon. Over twenty men could be seen running along the clifftop, heading in their direction. "They must have set off without Hogni, damn them" cursed Grimsson. "We must stand and fight. If they catch up with us alongside the boat, they will be able to pick us off individually with spears and arrows from the shore, and we will be hard-pressed to defend ourselves. Skjald-borg!" he rasped, giving the order to form the shield wall.

The point on the river where Bjorn's party and the boat lay, had a small overhang of rock, which narrowed the rough pathway. It was evident to all that this was the best point to defend without discussion. The boat lay across the path behind them as they watched the approaching warband. Grimsson instructed Bjorn and his three companions to mount the rock as a vantage point to throw spears and fire the bows that the party had brought from the Althing. He privately thought it better that those not specifically

trained as warriors did this task, at a distance
from their opponents, rather than be a weak link
in the defensive shield wall below on the path.
He glanced back to gauge the possibility of
escape down the river to the sea. It was not
good. Always supposing they were able to
launch the boat into the swollen river, it was still
a long way down to the sea, with rocks and
debris on the way, even if they could fight off
their fast approaching pursuers. As he looked
and thought, his eye was drawn to the prow of
the boat, pointing towards the water.

A long mooring rope hung from it for hauling it in
or out of the water. The line lay across the snow-
covered track as a narrow black line. Grimsson's
eyes widened, and he glanced skywards. "The
dark line in the snow – you were right Volva
Hrefna" he muttered. The others eyed him
sideways, with their primary attention on their
pursuers who had just reached the waterfall at
the ridge top. A flash of inspiration came.
Running back, Grimsson drew his sword and
chopped through the rope. "Come with me" he
barked at Sigurd and Sorli. They tied the line to a
tree trunk on the riverside of the track at knee
height. The tree was about thirty paces in front of
their shield wall. They ran the remainder of the
line down the tree trunk and across the track,
covering it in loose snow. The far end of the rope
was fed around a rocky outcrop, and back

towards the back of the overhanging rock on which the archers were standing.

"Don't pull it until they nearly reach it. Listen for my shout" Grimsson instructed. "Then re-join the shield wall." The rest of the party had already formed this; each man's shield butting up to the next, with just heads and spears protruding from the top. It looked threatening, but Grimsson had already calculated that they were heavily outnumbered. The pursuers would be attacking with the added impetus of charging downhill. Maybe the rope would use their own force against themselves, but the chances were that they would slow down as they approached. Re-joining his other men, he told them what to do. "Goad them into anger – An angry man is not so effective." This was something they had all learnt in training sessions and knew to be true. He continued giving some instructions, as much to still the fears of the younger untried men as having any hope of creating strategies. Rolph, as his most experienced man, did his bit to encourage the others to. "Remember," he said, trying to sound confident "we all have been trained well for this situation. Our master the Gothi has looked after us well with food, drink and clothes as well as good weapons, helmets and shields. Now is your chance to repay him."

Their pursuers re-emerged from the bend in the river track and as feared, slowed to almost stopping. At a nod and a murmured "Til-búinn"

ready command, the men in Grimsson's shield
wall began to bang their weapons against their
shields in what was hoped to be an intimidating,
aggravating gesture. "Stoppa! Go back!"
commanded Grimsson above the din, in a show
of confidence and bravado he did not feel "or die
at our hands! I dedicate the fallen to Odin." With
this, he stepped back from the line and
deliberately launched a spear over their heads in
an ancient ritual action to encourage the god's
help.

One or two of Hogni's men openly laughed at
such a display from an inferior foe. Still, others
were less sure of what was to come and
remembered how before conversion to the new
religion they had dedicated the dead to Odin with
a spear. What was more, several warily eyed the
legendary berserker Grettir Onundarson, who
was biting the top of his shield and growling like
some mad dog about to be unleashed.

Sensing a loss of control if he delayed much
longer, the leading man screamed "What are we
waiting for? We must avenge the insult to Hogni
and show we are not afraid of their outdated
superstitions. Come on!" With that the group
charged headlong down the slope towards
Grimsson's men, screaming a her-óp war whoop
"Árás!" the word for an attack, to give them
courage. Sigurd and Sorli, hidden around the
corner of the great rock did not have a good
view, but heard their master's loud yell and

hauled the rope taut just in time. There was a flurry of curses, screams and clashing metal as the attackers sprawled headlong over the now revealed rope, or collided with men who already had. Grimsson's men needed no orders now. Spears were thrown thick and fast so that some of the fallen were impaled on the ground beneath them. From the rock above, Bjorn and his friends loosed several volleys of arrows, picking off several more with deadly accuracy. Sigurd and Sorli re-joined the shield wall.

Those of Hogni's men who had not been in the front rank saw the slaughter and regrouped behind their shields. Their opponents had just enough spears left for one more volley, but their own had been mainly dropped in the red-stained snow. "Ready together" cried Grimsson, looking to his archers as well. "Now!" he shouted. His men threw their spears to hit at waist height. Their opponents instinctively lowered their shields to protect themselves, just as the last flight of arrows whistled down from a high angle at their less protected heads and shoulders. More men fell. Trying to take advantage of the onslaught, Grimsson led his men in a steady line up the hill to the dozen remnants, who had just witnessed an equal number of their comrades killed very effectively in front of them. Several had escaped arrows and spears hitting them, but had spears weighing down their shields, making them too unwieldy to hold or move. They dare not stop to pull them out with their enemy charging them, and some even discarded their shields rather than be handicapped by them.

Just before the two lines clashed, Grimsson shouted "Frey!" at the top of his voice. Frey is a Vanir fertility god with a boar as his symbol. The well-trained men fell into the Svínfylking boars-snout formation, an arrowhead with two men at its' point. The two were Grimsson himself and Onundarson, to punch through the defensive line of their adversaries. If one fell, the next man to him would assume his place so that the formation was maintained, and the momentum continued.

Holding his red-painted shield Grimsson struck out with his sword, and his men followed example with specifically aimed hits to the heads, shoulders and thighs of their enemies, who had their middles mainly covered by shields. Of course, many of their opponents had practised the same drills, and knew the appropriate blocking moves to meet these attacks and retaliated with each man trying to outguess the other as to which move would follow next. If an opening was left, a thrust might be made, and Sorli was lucky early on to kill his first man ever that way. Rolph and Atli swiftly dispatched the two opponents who had discarded shields and not found others to pick up on the flanks.

The line of Hogni's men broke, with one man shamefully trying to run away. Sigurd caught him with a sword stroke across his back that nearly cut him in two. Meanwhile, Grimsson had got another man backed up to a rock. Usually, you can step back to help counter a blow and cause your opponent to overreach, but the trapped man had no such option and fell crushed by Sven's shield being used as a battering ram weapon against him, and a fast-moving sword that snaked around the side and cut his thigh to the bone. As he fell, the sword plunged once more into his neck, and he breathed no more.

Seeing two men in front of him, Onundarson charged, flailing his favourite battle-axe. In panic they dived to the left and right before him, over-awed by this professional killer. He could not stop himself on the slippery ice and skidded through the middle of them. One slashed out with his sword as the old berserker's back was exposed on the way past. It was a deadly wound to the back, but he still swung his axe into the man's waist as he fell, killing him instantly. The other one of the pair used the advantage of the old man being on the ground to thrust his sword through his neck but had no chance relish the killing. As he straightened a whirling demon of flesh and metal ran towards him, screaming. It was the fallen berserker's son Hamdir, with another war axe.

The rest of the force had been killed, except for one young boy who had run back up the hill, doubtlessly to report back. Nearly all of Grimsson's men watched in silence as the last two adversaries met. Hamdir tried to pull the man's shield down by hooking the bottom bearded end of his axe over it, but this proved futile as his opponent backed off breaking free each time. The man aimed a couple of blows, which clashed against Hamdir's shield boss, but then went for a cleaving blow to the head. Hamdir's regular sparring partners grinned when they saw how he had blocked it with the shaft of his axe held horizontally above his head, with the axe head pointing off to Hamdir's right side. They had practised often enough with Hamdir to know the move he usually made next from that position. His opponent did not. Using the sword as a pivot, Hamdir swung the axe head round like a spoke on a cartwheel, with the man's sword as the upright axle. It divided the man's jaw from the rest of his skull and cut the top of the neck clean through. There was a showering of blood covering Hamdir's helm and shield as he looked down upon the decapitated corpse of the man who had killed his father.

Grimsson was not sure of what to say as he stepped up to Hamdir, but as he did, the words came. "I am sorry that your father is gone, but he will be glad that he has gone straight to Valhalla. He will be glad to witness your prowess as a warrior with his favourite weapon, the axe. Pick his weapon up now and bring it with you – it is yours by right, and you have proven today that you are your father's son." Hamdir bowed his head, picked up his father's axe and strolled to his group of comrades. They patted his back and stood in a collective embarrassed silence until Grimsson bustled up. "We will send men back to bury Onundarson. Gather any useful swords and get the boat launched quickly before a larger force arrives." Glad of an action to get them out of an awkward situation the men set to with a will to drag the boat into the swirling waters of the river. It was difficult, especially as they were all tired with the exertions of the battle and their flight from the Althing beforehand.

The boat was overloaded, and water lapped over the sides onto the thirteen men who crowded in, together with their weaponry and that which they had collected. There was Grimsson, his six housecarls, Bjorn and his three friends doing the rowing with the only four oars plus the two servants. The boat was only designed to hold four to six fishermen, their catch and nets.

Right from the start, the rowers had difficulty in steering a middle course down the flooded river and avoiding banks, rocks and debris, and the others tried to help by also hanging onto their oars with them. Everyone was soaked very quickly, and shivering set in from the combined effects of the cold and their recent skirmish.

They did not need to propel themselves with the oars. Instead, they tried to use them to help correct the erratic course, and to fend off larger debris in the water, such as logs. Water flowed over the sides of the overloaded boat almost continuously, so that two of the men had to bale it out with their helmets.

Fortunately, none were seriously injured, although almost all had minor cuts and bruises. The craft bucked like an untrained horse and twisted like an unwilling woman, but still, they clung on, peering through the spray for the river mouth. All of a sudden it was upon them, as the sea's waves hit the river's water spewing into it. The boat reared up, and at that moment a tree trunk was spotted directly beneath them. They came down with a rending crash upon it, and it burst through the bottom planks more powerfully than any sword thrust they had just witnessed. It was every man for himself as the craft capsized. Some clung to the upturned hull while others gripped the treacherous tree trunk. The weight of Grimsson's chain mail impeded him, but firm hands hauled him from the water onto the half-submerged hull.

The water was freezing, and all knew they would not survive long in it. The buffeting of large waves continued to make their task of clinging on the more difficult. Fortunately, both wind and tide were driving them towards the shore, but it was still some way off, and the shattered boat heaved in a drunken, circular motion that dizzied the senses and sought to loosen the grip of frozen, aching hands. Some could not swim, and Grimsson's mail coat would weigh him down to the seabed if he ventured into the sea with it on, yet it was difficult enough for someone to remove it over his head on firm dry land, let alone an unstable upturned boat. The ignominy of surviving the battle yet perishing at sea weighed heavy.

Just then, Bjorn shouted. A female figure could be seen on the shore. It was his elderly mother, the fish curer. She waved, then ran back towards her hut in the distance, and after what seemed an age threw a dark shape towards the sea. It was a long fishing net, with floats, and it drifted agonisingly slowly towards them but was washed back frequently towards the shore by the waves.

A faint howling was heard on the wind. It was an unearthly, primal scream that added, even more, shivers to each man. They peered up through the spray to see another female figure on the high ground. Her arms were upstretched to the sky, and her long grey hair was streaming into the wind. There was no mistaking the figure of the Volva Hrefna. Even as they watched, the sea around them calmed as the wind dropped. Of course, it might have done that naturally, but there were no doubts in any of the men's minds of the timing of such a coincidence, with the added wonderment of how on earth she always knew where and when to arrive when things were happening. She was doing her bit to help, and as the waves decreased the fishing net cast by Bjorn's mother glided over the wave crests towards them little by little.

At length, one of the servants clinging to the log caught an end, and the other occupants kicked out with their legs to drive them to the upturned hull. Willing but frozen hands grabbed it and slowly hauled hand over hand towards the shore. It took a long time, and the net was nearly lost once due to sheer exhaustion, but finally, the shallow shelving beach was reached, and they dragged themselves thankfully to dry land, abandoning the hull and tree trunk to the surf.

Bjorn hugged his mother, who scolded him for such foolhardiness in attempting the trip. The others leaned on each other in exhaustion; amused to see the grown man reduced to a scared youth by one so small of stature. They all thanked her and Hrefna, and she got out the ox and cart used to transport the fish so that they could get back to Sven's farm sooner, wrapped in rough fishy sacks to beat the cold that had set in. Hrefna offered some flatbread to eat, together with some herbs to stave off the effects of the cold. They chewed into them and gagged at their bitterness, but she stood there imperiously, daring with her gaze any man not to take some before departing. They meekly obeyed like scolded puppies.

They were not cheered on their rattling oxcart journey by the reflection of Sigurd, who had been maintaining that he recognised the last man Hamdir had killed. "I know it!" he exclaimed. "I knew I recognised him from somewhere. I remember now. He was at the Althing beside Hogni. It was his son." There was a small groan. Hogni would be out for an act of double revenge when he found out that, and the party continued it's slow and bone jolting progress up the icy track, inland to the west of the Ytri-Ranga river. They did not have to take the longer route that had led Bjorn to discovering the body, because it was a bit safer for the ox cart to cross the swollen ford over the river towards the village of Oddi than a lone man.

The ride seemed inexorably long, and the ox refused to move quicker than its accustomed slow pace. They all were aware that they might be too late to save the farm if Hogni reached it first, although their route had been quicker than his presumed course over the icy roads, particularly if he had men on foot. However, as they approached, they could see a band of men milling around the farm.

Chapter 10

Relief was on every man's face as they drew nearer to the farmstead, and they could pick out individual men who had arrived from the outlying tenant farms. Some came to meet them, waving weapons in their hands, though Grimsson sourly but silently noticed they held them awkwardly or were only equipped with sickles and kitchen knives. The men parted as Aud and her daughter Gudrun caught up and pushed their way through.

"You're soaked!" said Aud, rather obviously, but not quite knowing how to greet her husband back from the dead, at least in her own mind. Turning, she shouted at the Thrall slaves. "Don't just stand there, gawking! Get dry clothes and hot food or at least soup for these men." Sometimes generating action is easier than exposing one's true feelings of relief, love, fear, anger and confusion. Gudrun was more direct. She simply ran at Hamdir and flung her arms around his neck, clutching to him grimly so that no one may take him away from her again. Hamdir stood rigid and uncertain, his arms wavering and embarrassment all over his face. He badly wanted to return her embrace but was aware that the eyes of everyone, including her father, was upon them. Her mother arched her eyebrows, saying nothing but looking intently towards her husband for a lead. Grimsson, at last, spoke; "Always a warm welcome!" he joked, indicating his wife and ducking his head and protecting it with his hands from an imagined clout from her. Waving vaguely towards his daughter and Hamdir, he simply added, "He deserves a hero's welcome. They all do." Clapping his hands to everyone to indicate his brief statement was over, and rapid action was expected, he strode towards Aud and enveloped her in a bear-like hug. His wet, fishy garb transferred its aura to her pristine apron, but for once she had no care for niceties and gave him a full kiss on the lips. There was a slight murmur of action around the couple, but they were lost in the moment until a somewhat less sensitive thrall interrupted with a bowl of hot soup and a large wooden spoon. Abandoning the implement, Grimsson just tipped the bowl back into his eager mouth, nearly scalding himself in the process. His comrades followed suit, before hurrying to the hall.

The Gothi's party barely had time to put on any dry clothes before a lad on the lookout on the track leading to the farmstead ran back panting to raise the alarm that Hogni's force was coming. The exhausted survivors of the shipwreck wearily formed another shield wall in front of the main hall, with servants and men from the other farms arranged on each flank. They had barely thirty men, many of whom were poorly equipped and untrained. To the right of them were the women's quarters and weaving room, to the left a barn and stable. It was a too large area to defend adequately, so Grimsson had decided to make his stand in one place rather than spread his meagre force too thin. He preferred to fight in the open rather than be caught inside the hall if it was set alight. The entrance to the farmstead was directly in front of them. Hogni's party looked to number about fifty. Although some of his men had been killed at the river, it was believed that a dozen or so of his well-equipped and trained housecarls had remained at the Althing to escort Hogni after the trial. Lesser-trained men joined these, but there was no shortage of weapons, whereas some of Grimsson's were merely armed with farm tools.

Grimsson did wonder how many of his enemies were supporting Hogni willingly, as opposed to doing it for fear or duty. He liked to think that his men thought well of him and would be loyal. Indeed, if Hogni were killed or injured early on, his men would be less likely to fight on enthusiastically. However, he couldn't recognise him in the crowd that marched to the entrance and started to funnel through to a ragged volley of spears and arrows from the small amount that was left. The new fashion of eye protection on the helmets made the enemy more anonymous, and few of the shields had any decoration. They were all very similar, brown leather over a round wooden frame with a central raised metal boss to protect the hand of the bearer. Grimsson noted with pride that two of his farmhand's sons, no more than twelve summers old, were enthusiastically letting fly with sling shots, which they whirled with high accuracy towards the oncoming enemy while remaining in cover behind the line. They did little damage to shield or armour, but a couple of un-armoured men went down with gashes to their heads, and others obviously found them a nuisance value diverting them from the focus of advancing on the line of warriors before them.

There was an unintelligible yell from the advancing enemy ranks, and they ran full tilt at the shield wall. "Hold steady" commanded Grimsson, as his spear connecting with an opponent's shield jarred his arm. The ash shaft shattered, so he switched to hacking over the top of his shield at the man's head with his sword. His opponent was well armoured and trained, and stepped back, putting Grimsson off balance as his sword sliced the air. As he hacked towards the man's right shoulder, his weapon was blocked by the other's vertical blade. There was a flash from Grimsson's left, as Sigurd who was next to him thrust a spear into the man's unprotected side. The comrades flashed each other a grim smile as the falling man was replaced with three more who stepped over his body to get at them.

On the barn end of the line, Bjorn appeared in a guise his friends had never really imagined. He was usually quiet and lacked confidence, but here he was now shouldering a small tree trunk, with the roots still attached, which he wielded like a club. As the enemy had advanced, his friends heard him be really angry almost for the first time. "I worked on that boat with my father before he died. It is all I have to remember him by and would have had lots of good fishing in it. It is their fault it is smashed. Now I am going to smash them!" He was no trained warrior, but long days hauling nets and lifting baskets of fish about had given him ample muscles to swing the tree as if it were no more than a demented dancing partner. His form loomed large over three opponents, each of whom thought he was some sort of berserker. While they were still goggling at him the tree whipped in arcs, scything them down like ripened barley. Encouraged by his example, his three friends from the boat crew exacted their own terrible revenge, stamping on the prostrate figures with force and hacking with boathook, sickle and an eating knife.

In the middle of the line, the housecarls around Grimsson were hard-pressed. The frequent sword drills and combat classes that they had endured could still not prepare them entirely for the heaving mass of hate that assailed them. The constant thuds of weapon against shield, and more occasional clanging of metal against metal disorientated the senses inside the confines of the metal helmets they wore. Like some vastly complicated game of king's table, each swing of an opponent's weapon must be met by a defence by blocking it with a sword or gradually splintering shield. Trying to double guess the next move to counter, and then to retaliate towards any exposed weak point became as much a trial for the brain as the arms and legs that weighed heavy with exhaustion.

The panting gasp, the wild eye beneath a visor and the grunts and muttered curses sung a dreadful litany of bold attack and fearful defence. Step forward and thrust or swing. Step back and parry the oncoming blow. Like two ends of a giant log saw, the two opposing lines oscillated as if the wood beneath it was too green or knotted to cut. Atli caught a blow to the centre of his helm that made his ears ring. Enraged, he found a sudden rush of adrenaline and surprised his red-headed adversary (who thought he had finished him) by slashing low at his legs as he stumbled. With a great yell, the man almost fell on top of him, but Atli managed to step back just in time to deliver a second decisive swipe at the fallen man's exposed neck, which nearly decapitated him. Atli registered a yell from Giuki at his left side, alerting him to an axe swinging at him from the other direction. There was no chance to celebrate one victory when a defeat was as likely to follow so quickly behind it. He parried the stroke with his shield, which finally gave up staying in one piece, and he was left with half of it attached to the handle he hung onto beneath the metal boss. Infuriated, but trying to maintain a calculated approach, he thrust the broken corner at the man's face and rammed it in his mouth more by chance than skill. His sword bit down onto the startled warrior's head, ensuring that his last meal was of wood and leather.

Out of the corner of his eye, he saw Sorli at his right shoulder, struggling to keep two men at bay at once. He was doing well, but with no one in front of him, Atli turned and closed his shattered shield edge to the one held by his comrade, in an attempt to help even the odds. It was deadly yet somewhat even struggle, as they tried to beat off Hogni's men together without getting in each other's way. Behind the pair of men facing them were more waiting their turn.

While the barn end of the line held firm, following Bjorn's shining example, the opposite end by the women's quarters was not faring so well under a concentrated assault by a superior force. Two of the poorly equipped men went down, and their dismayed comrades fell back to almost behind the line of housecarls. At the end of that line was Hamdir, who despite exhaustion was fighting well. He knew that the eyes of the women (including Gudrun) would be peeking through holes in their building's wall. What he didn't realise was Aud's firm words to the women beforehand: "Put away your weaving – we will weave a knife through the first of Hogni's men who try and enter here." Although afraid, each had taken up a shearing tool, kitchen knife or sickle."

They looked on in horrible fascination, as two men advanced on Hamdir, who was holding his father's great axe. He met the first square on with his shield, barging him into the other. While they struggled to regain balance, his axe sliced sideways into the first man's shoulder, momentarily unprotected as he dropped his shield low to duck away. A gush of blood shot out as the man screamed out in pain and terror, stumbling away, clutching his shoulder and dropping his guard altogether. Two farm hands saw their chance and darted out with a rake and spade every bit as deadly when embedded into your back. Meanwhile, Hamdir was being beaten back by the other warrior, who was experienced at the art of killing. To his left, he heard Atli call out that it looked as though reinforcements were entering the yard. But this was not the only threat to him.

Making his way around the back of the hall, past Grimsson's bathing pool, was Hogni and five of his men. They had hung back from the main party and circled around unnoticed by the beleaguered force at the front of the hall. The intention was to get behind the flank, and it looked as though there was to be a bonus. "Leave that one to me!" whispered Hogni, indicating the back of Hamdir. "He killed my son." He approached quietly and cautiously in a crouched style, with a giant axe raised to strike. Concentrating on staying alive with his primary aggressor in front of him, Hamdir was oblivious to the threat from behind.

The door opened a small amount in the women's quarters. Suddenly Hogni had three arrows sticking out of his back and side and was falling forward. Hamdir's opponent, who had been aware of the attack coming from the rear of his adversary, was shocked to see his lord fall. In that instant of indecision, Hamdir's axe swung low, cutting deep into his thigh. The follow-up thrust into the chest was in almost before the fellow hit the ground.

It was if the battle was frozen at that moment. Hogni could be seen dead on the ground by most of his men, plus all those of Grimsson who were on that side of the hall. Their heads swung like curious cattle, to see which unexpected point the arrows had come from. Their eyes fixed upon a well-rounded figure of a young woman, standing in the open doorway of the women's quarters. The bow was still in her hand, and the expression on Gudrun's face was a mixture of hatred and defiance. Her mother, Aud, rushed to her trembling side to pull her behind the door before she was attacked. No attack came. The survivors of Hogni's force backed away from the line. It was then that Grimsson realised the extra factor that was helping them decide their futures. Lined up across the entrance were thirty more men, with Budli Arnason at their centre. Yes, there were reinforcements, but they were for Grimsson. Some had arrows and spears levelled at the remnant of Hogni's force, whilst the others stood with swords and shields in their hands.

"Stoppa! Let them go!" commanded Grimsson. He saw no logic in getting more men killed or maimed when the cause was removed from life. His demoralised opponents backed away slowly, keeping their guard up and not losing eye contact until they were down the road. Arnason made a gap in his line for them to pass through, and it was evident that he would have any man killed who tried to restart the quarrel. They took a dozen severely wounded men with them, but left twelve dead behind, including Hogni. Rolph stepped forward to stop a couple of hotheads pursuing them. He was bleeding badly from a wound to his cheek. Remarkably, only two men had died of Grimsson's force. Several had terrible injuries but would survive.

Arnason stepped forward, and Grimsson greeted him warmly. "Thank you for coming to my assistance. I hope you will not think ill of me if I say it was unexpected?"

"Not at all" replied Budli Arnason. "It is true we are of different religions, but I would rather have an honourable heathen as a friend than a false-hearted Christian. I do not see why we cannot live peaceably side by side. I am sorry that I did not arrive earlier, but by the time I found out the plans of Hogni and mustered my men much time had passed. Mind you; it seems as though you have had excellent help from your daughter" he said, nodding towards the women's quarters, where the occupants were filing out of the door so recently used by Gudrun.

Grimsson visibly swelled with pride, but then suddenly realised he was failing in his duties of hospitality, and apologised, offering whatever food and drink could be mustered. Arnason gracefully and politely declined.

"You have some sorting out to do. I will be glad to accept an invitation when you have buried the dead and taken care of the living." With that, he led his men away, leaving the Gothi to ponder what to do next.

It was at this point that Aud resumed control of her household, bellowing orders for the care of the wounded. Grimsson moved inside the hall and sat down heavily on a bench. His head ached from the blows to his helmet, and both his sword and shield arms felt as if they were as heavy as iron. His legs ached, and his neck and back were stiff. A hand rested on his shoulder from behind. It was Aud. She didn't say anything, but gently led him to their chamber, and helped him off with his mail shirt and boots. "Rest now, my love. It is all under control. You really had me worried this time."

Grimsson leaned back with a sigh on the bed. "I'm getting too old for all of this. But don't tell anyone, will you?" he grinned, turning over and falling almost instantly into a deep sleep. Aud pulled a fur over his bulky form, kissed the top of his balding head gently, and quietly left the chamber. He slept until late the next morning and awoke to find fresh clothes laid out beside him. He still ached but felt refreshed. Some bread and goat's milk cheese was swiftly eaten, alongside a horn cup of ale. He was just about to busy himself finding out what injuries had been received or damage done when his wife appeared. "Go and have a good soak in that bathing pool first" she commanded. "And while you are there you can think about what you will have to do next. Meanwhile, I expect you will want a feast tomorrow, or the day after, so I'd better be off and organise it." With that, she was gone, almost before he had indicated he would prefer two days. Her leaving left him shaking his head ruefully. Being outnumbered two to one in a battle was one thing, but trying to argue against Aud when she was organising was as much use as a spear made of milk.

Chapter 11

Later, Grimsson made a point of talking to everyone still on the farm. The tenants had left to get back to tending their farms, taking some wounded and the two dead men with them. He sent word to them and Arnason to return for a feast in two days. He promised Hamdir to accompany him to the River Thjorsa battle site tomorrow, to perform a burial rite for his father. He also looked him straight in the eye, stretched out a hand onto his shoulder and gruffly said, "You have my permission to court Gudrun." Hamdir thanked him for both blessings and asked whether he thought the axe should go into the mound.

After pausing for thought, Grimsson pronounced; "It is up to you, but I know your father was a practical man. I am sure he would rather his son use it to such good effect. I am sure they will have plenty of axes available for him in Valhalla."

As he went around, he praised anyone from thrall to housecarl that had helped in any way and promised them all a tasty feast. He didn't forget the two slingshot lads either and told them they had the right attitude to become great housecarls as they grew older. If they were prepared to practice hard, he would see to it that they received suitable training. Their looks of sheer joy told him their answer more eloquently with the excited, garbled words that poured out of them.

Fortunately, not too much damage had been sustained by the buildings. Two chickens and some crushed eggs were the only other loss. Virtually all his housecarls had suffered some wounds, but the Volva had appeared, distributing poultices, herbs and healing, and assured him that none would die. She waived the right to any ceremonial welcome but said she would stop for the feast. He praised them all for their efforts.

Finally, he came to his daughter Gudrun. She wasn't quite so confident now and lowered her eyes in expectation of a severe telling off in her actions towards Hamdir, if not the marksmanship with the bow. He hated to see his daughter fear him, and for once could imagine the turmoil of thoughts and feelings coursing through her. "Come here to your father," he said simply, opening his arms wide. She came right up to him and was enfolded in them. "The young girl who could fight with staves and compete at archery with the boys has not forgotten her skills as she becomes a woman so rapidly before my eyes it seems" he smiled, trying to allay her fears. "I was so frightened for you when you killed Hogni yesterday" he continued, "but so proud as well. You may have made a few errors of judgement in how you acted with Hamdir, but as far as I am concerned your demonstration of troth cancels everything out.

Much rubbish has been spoken about troth, but it comes down to standing by your kin and acting honourably, whatever the personal cost. You have done that twice in the space of a week, and

I commend you for it." Realising the end of his statement sounded a bit pompous, Grimsson smiled and added, "Now if you can give your old father a kiss, we'll see if you can't make the rest of Hamdir's life a misery!" He laughed uproariously at his own joke. It wasn't that it was superbly funny; it was just a great relief to show any sort of emotion after the last few days. Gudrun started as she realised what her father was implying and joined in the laughter and planted a kiss on his whiskery cheek. They continued talking for some time. It was the most extended, frankest conversation they had enjoyed together for years, and the Gothi was pleased for once he didn't feel embarrassed or at such a loss around female emotions. This is how things should be, he decided.

The next day, Grimsson and Aud, Hamdir and a party of men and women went back to the river to bury Grettir Onundarson in a mound overlooking the sea, with full ceremony. The Gothi hallowed the ground with his Thorshammer, and nine girls, representing the wave maidens tossed scarves of blue material in the air to represent the Berserker's last journey to Valhalla, accompanied by a portion of meat and mead. Grimsson intoned the traditional verse, extolling the fact that a man lived on by the reputation he left behind him;

Cattle die, kinsmen die, dies oneself the same;
But a glorious reputation never dies

For whoever gets for himself a good one.

They all shivered in the breeze blowing off the river on their return. Quietly reflecting that it was probably an excellent orlög luck, built up by their family for generations that had enabled any to survive that fateful day, either in battle or on that treacherous, foaming tumult of melted ice.

The next day, the tenants and their men re-appeared, together with Arnason and half a dozen of his men. The smell of roasting meat filled the air and mingled with the smell of bean broth and fresh bread. There were salted fish and a curdled milk drink to, but most men's eyes were on the barrels of ale and mead brought out of the store. In deference to Arnason's beliefs, the Gothi held a simple ceremony of thanks to the Gods and Goddesses in advance of his men and the women entering the hall. Thanks were offered to Odin, Thor and Frey in particular, and their statues gleamed in the firelight, reflecting dappled light onto the offerings of food and drink laid before them.

In the women's quarters, Aud led the singing of a chant, with Volva Hrefna joining in with a flat but loud voice that carried over the voices of the other women so loudly that Gudrun had to suppress a giggle. It was a release from the constant comments from the others, ranging from praise for her bravery and accuracy, to censure for her foolhardiness and lack of womanly virtues. She was tempted to snap back at such comments but resisted in the knowledge that she knew she'd done the right thing and that some of the petty bickering came from jealousy.

Her mother remained aloof, knowing that there were some things her daughter had to work out for herself independently, although she would be ready with advice and support if she asked. Instead, she beamed a steady proud smile at her, in the reassurance of her general approval, and a small plan came into her head to silence the gossips and show her thoughts without descending to their level.

Finally, when all the guests were seated, Aud went amongst them with a large, decorated drinking horn of mead. She started with her husband, then Arnason and Volva Hrefna as the most honoured guests, and then worked her way around the descending ranks of people. At this stage, she slowly and deliberately went over to her daughter Gudrun, (knowing that all eyes were on her) and placed a second horn into her hands to assist. This was a rare honour since the privilege resided with the head of the household. Yet, everyone could see that she was honouring her daughter for her recent actions, and maybe preparing her for the time when she would possibly take over some of her mother's Gytha priestess duties. In any case, all smiled and nodded encouragement. Even with two mead horn bearers, the process took a long time, as each person gathered tilted back their head for a swig before handing back the horn with a loud 'Waes Hael!" well-wishing or individual toast to Grimsson and his warriors. Arnason and Grimsson themselves had diplomatically toasted each other and the assembled crowd to start with.

Then it was the turn of the slaves to bring in the food. Great wooden bowls of bean broth and flatbread were consumed as everyone exchanged tales of their experiences in the last week. Some men were modest, while others boasted of their heroic deeds, egging each other on to exaggerate every blow, the size, ferocity and quantity of the enemy. The talk subdued, and a cheer went up as a whole sheep, and whole pig were delivered on poles into the hall by some sweating thralls. They were delivered to the top table where Arnason, the housecarls and the two tenant farmers flanked Grimsson, Aud, Hrefna and Gudrun.

Arnason had already relayed on the verdict of the Althing; that Grimsson was to receive one of Hogni's minor farms. His widow would inherit Hogni's main one since their son had died. As men got to the stage of gnawing the bones of the meat that had been on their wooden platters, Grimsson rose to his feet and banged his red, battle-scarred shield hanging on the wall behind him. The noise subsided as he spoke.

"We have all been through some hard times recently. This feast is to thank every one of you for your help and support. Firstly, let me thank my honoured guest Budli Arnason and his men. We have our differences of opinion over some things, but we agree on the important ones, such as honour and dealing honestly with people." He paused to let this sink in and was pleased to see his rehearsed words seemed well received. "Secondly, I must thank my beautiful wife, the Gytha Aud Harnsdottir, for her wise counsel and organisation of this wonderful feast." There was much banging on the table at this. The food was superb. "I must also not forget my courageous housecarls, tenants and everyone else who fought at my side, not forgetting Bjorn, who I saw in a new light. I will be providing him with all the timber and materials he needs to build another boat. The difference will be that he will own it himself and may trade as he sees fit. We cannot have such a dangerous man around this place, especially if he finds any more bodies!" The hall laughed at the grim joke, and Bjorn simply bowed his head towards his ex-master in thanks and embarrassment. While this was going on the Gothi whispered to a servant to fetch the small treasure chest from his chamber. When it arrived on the floor beside him, he asked his wife to open it with the key she had suspended from her girdle hanger; an anchor-shaped piece of metal hung from her brooch. With the small chest open towards him, he called his housecarls to line up in front of him.

"For their valiant service, I am giving five of them silver from my hoard" he announced. The men's eyes glistened, not just at his generosity but at the enhancement of their reputations in such a public way. Smiling, their leader continued. "As some of you know, my daughter has shown great bravery to, but is far too dangerous a burden for any ordinary man." He paused for effect, a twinkle in his eye for Gudrun. "So, I must entrust her to Hamdir, who is likely to get an arrow in him if he annoys her in any way!" Hamdir was struck dumb, his mouth open. Gudrun squealed with delight, hugged her mother, father and finally Hamdir, to much cheering and laughter. "Since they are both so dangerous, I will give Hamdir Hogni's old farm, which I have just acquired as the bride price. It is far enough away so that we will not have to hear them fighting!" He roared at his own joke and was joined by the others.

With this, the other housecarls banged Hamdir on the back and hoisted him on their shoulders around the hall. Even though they would have all liked to have wed Gudrun, they were glad for their comrade's good fortune. Then there were more toasts of ale and mead, including ones between Arnason and Grimsson swearing troth bonds of friendship. As celebratory platters of stewed puffins and slatur were brought in (made of offal, blood, fat and meat sewn into a sheep's stomach), a skald started a ballad, hurriedly composed to detail and celebrate the recent victory. It was in one of the old metre forms, and many were quite moved at its alliteration, and the kennings that likened the shield wall to a fighting stallion, and Gudrun to a Valkyrie.

Finally, the six housecarls gathered together, shaking away their drunkenness to perform a victory dance. They had put on decorated helmets, representing the bear, wolf and aurochs, a mighty bison only found in the land of their forefathers. Each had two spears, and they shuffled in a line around the room to the steady beating of hands and platters on the tables, and the pulse of rock drums made from worn grinding bowls covered with hide. A lighter rhythm came from a couple of rattles made from hardened bulls' testicles. The arms bearing the spears were held painfully out to their sides, level with their shoulders. Even small children allowed up late on this special occasion and peeking nervously from their mother's skirts clapped their hands and bobbed in time to the monotonous but hypnotic rhythm. The dancers formed two lines of three and advanced and retreated from each other with spears held in mock threat, and wild cries. First, they clashed their own pair of spears, and then those of the other dancers. All the time their feet stamped out a defiant beat, which they added to with the butt end of the spears occasionally.

Then they turned outwards and charged their audience, stopping just short and driving their spearheads to the ground a hand's width in front of folk's toes. In this they showed their accuracy as well as power, before turning back into a circle, clashing each pair of spears in time. Then they clashed their own spears, followed by those of their now sweat streaked neighbours, criss-crossing the circle in opposing pairs. It took practice, agility and quickness of mind, and no one was left in doubt as to the quality of their skill and training, least of all the young women who gasped, clapped and cheered their particular favourites. It was said by some afterwards that only Hamdir went to bed alone that night, in respect of his forthcoming wedding.

Within a month, Sven Grimsson and Aud had proudly performed the wedding of their only daughter, placing the symbolic Thorshammer into her lap, as she bowed her head beneath a veil, her lengthy hair gathered up in a married woman's tidier hairstyle.

Olaf Tryggvason of Norway died later that year to be succeeded by his son Olaf the Second, who continued converting his people to Christianity forcibly. In Denmark, Harald Bluetooth was taking a similar line, and both put

Iceland under pressure to convert to their Christian religion.

In the meantime, Grimsson and Arnason had returned to the end session of the Althing to join in the debate regarding the future official religion of Iceland. While previously they may have been expected to oppose each other, instead they made a joint suggestion to the assembly; that although Christianity be adopted, those who wished to, could still honour the old gods in the privacy of their own household. It did not go down well with Gissur the White and his party who wanted complete conversion to Christianity. His son Isleifur later became the first new Icelandic Christian priest.

When Thorgeir Thorkelson was entrusted by the Althing to make a pronouncement on the matter, he went and meditated in privacy and darkness beneath some animal skins for two whole days. On his return, he announced that Grimsson and Arnason's idea would be the one adopted since it allowed the individual freedoms fiercely enjoyed by Icelanders, whilst also giving a consensus between men who respected each other's right to be different. The eating of horseflesh was still to be allowed. On his way home he hurled his small statues of the old gods into the mighty bubbling cauldron of a waterfall near his home. It is known to this day as Gothafoss, 'The Fall of the Gods', and the walls

of water that hurtle down between the black
rocks still hiss and froth with their spirits.

What the hell do you mean?

(Originating from another challenge to write a story in less than 300 words.)

"What the hell do you mean?"

"If you don't know by now, I have given up explaining."

Typical comeback from her when she can't be arsed to argue. Just leave the statement there to fester then. I got out of the chair and took a walk down the garden. Brown leaves, cat crap and the evidence of another failed plan to do something constructive. I frowned, and lashed out at a marauding moth, and got even grumpier when I missed. Sod it. I'll go to bed early for a change.

She came up much later. I pretended to be asleep while she slid her icy body between the duvet and two-toned fitted sheet. Her choice obviously. Another not so subtle change she thought she'd sneaked in bellow the radar. Why are women's bodies always cold? They panic about fat then complain about keeping warm all the time. I rested my hand heavily on the edge of the duvet on my side, to make sure she didn't hog it in the night.

The uneasy armed truce continued at breakfast. "Have we any marmalade left?"

"No, you got through that last jar in no time. Better get some when you go shopping." She knows I hate food shopping. That night on the way home from work I got some, the dark chunky stuff she doesn't like. I also chucked in some Red Gloucester cheese, bourbon biscuits, tinned rice pudding and a pepperoni pizza she wouldn't like, as well as the usual weekly stuff.

She didn't say anything as I unpacked the carrier bags, just sniffed with attitude and avoided meeting my eyes. Hers were pink and puffy, just like the colour coordinated pillows.

Dark Ages Slavery

Written for the Ealdfaeder website
www.ealdfaeder.org

Late Roman period

The slave keeping Romans had to contend with
Saxon pirates raiding England and taking away
goods and slaves. Saint Patrick, a Romano-
Briton, was said to have been taken to Ireland
for six years in that way before escaping back to
England. Those Saxons became the next wave
of settlers, in conflict with the Britons remaining
after the Romans had left.

Anglo Saxon Slavery

It may be an uncomfortable fact, but Anglo
Saxons and the Viking races thought that slavery
was a regular part of their working economy. It
has been estimated from entries in the
Doomsday Book that as much as 10% of the
population of Anglo Saxon England were slaves.
This is difficult to verify, as one has to estimate
the size of slave families from the actual working
slaves listed. The term þeowen denoted female
slave, and þeowincel a little or young slave. The
general Old English term for a slave was wealh,
which is associated with the ideas of 'Welsh' or
'foreigner.' That gives a clue to one of the
significant sources of slaves: prisoners of war.

To give some examples: Earl Godwin enslaved followers of Alfred the Aethling in 1036, Earl Harold took slaves in his raid on the West Country in 1052, and Earl Morcar took hundreds of slaves in Northamptonshire in 1065. In the late 12th century King David of Scotland captured so many slaves on a raid into England that it was said that every Scottish household had one.

William of Malmesbury describes young men and women bound with ropes at the port of Bristol, and other centres of slave trade included Carbridge in the North. Slaves are sometimes described as being in chains. While a metal neck collar was sometimes used to denote that someone was a slave, it seems that generally that they were only kept in chains as punishment. One badge of a free-born person was to wear a knife, so this was forbidden to slaves. However, trusted slaves must have been allowed to use a knife to do some types of work.

Slaves may have worked at ploughing, building walls, spreading muck, peat digging, grinding corn, dairy duties cooking or general housework. However, higher status occupations are recorded, such as goldsmith or embroiderer. Some female slaves were used as sex workers, although later laws tried to protect female slaves from sexual abuse. There is a record of the sister of the Danish King Cnut selling girls from England to Denmark. Cnut himself passed a law that a man would forfeit a female slave he committed adultery with and Christian Penitentials such as Theodore's ordered that a master must fast for a year and free a slave woman that he had got pregnant.

Manumission

The Christian exhortation to free slaves must have been controversial, if not hypocritical since some clergy employed slaves on their estates, and monasteries often depended upon them. However, Bede records in Historia Ecclesiastica that Bishop Wilfred freed 250 slaves at the land he was given at Selsey in the 7th century. There was an agreement at the Synod of Chelsea in 816 that one slave would be freed by each bishop when one of their fellow bishops died. The churchman Wulfstan condemns the practice of Anglo Saxons selling their countrymen abroad to Pagans in his Sermo ad Lupi (c.1014 AD) and blames the rule of the foreign king (Cnut) on God's displeasure at the practice. He and other bishops urged that slaves be allowed Sundays off to pursue their own activities, and be allowed to observe fasts and that they should be beaten if they did not follow them (since they were unlikely to have money to pay a fine like their masters.)

Giving up one's slaves (sometimes known as manumission) may have been hard to contemplate: who else was going to plough the fields, cook, or herd the pigs, while the landowner got on with higher status tasks like weaving, trading or warfare? Inevitably, some Anglo Saxons converted to Christianity made provision in their wills for freeing their slaves when they died, so that they could continue to use them in the meantime. To give a slave their freedom involved taking them to a church and handing them over to the priest, who then led them around the altar three times and said some words. There are references to slaves being freed at crossroads, which probably reflects the Germanic practices (formulated in a Lombard law) which includes giving the slave an arrow and a whip and letting them decide which one of the roads to take.

Other sources of slavery

There were a few different ways that people may end up as slaves, other than as prisoners of war: the Old English term wite þeow refers to penal enslavement, i.e. punishment of a court for a crime. Some families who had become bankrupt may sell their children, or even themselves to ensure survival, and in some cases, they were allowed to earn money to redeem themselves, and repay their price or debt. Such slaves were termed nidþeowas.

One source quotes the price of slaves as 306 grams of silver (male) and 204 grams (female). Those prices are the equivalent today of approximately £3950 & £2630. How that would compare with engaging a paid servant and keeping them in food and accommodation over the same period I do not know. Another 10th-century source (the agreement between Anglo Saxons and the Celtic Dunsæte tribe) puts the price of a slave at one pound of silver, compared to 1.50 pounds of silver for a horse, as a comparison. However, some manumissions indicate a half-pound in weight of silver as the going rate for a slave's freedom.

Viking Slave Trade

The term that Vikings used for slavery was generally ánauð and a slave was referred to as a þral or thrall. One could be termed a fostne, which indicated that you were a hereditary fostered slave. Bond servants (Bondi) could pay off their owner if they could raise enough money. The image of a slave was one who had short-cropped hair and an iron neck collar. After Christianisation, a female slave was not allowed to wear a kerchief over her hair, which was a privilege reserved for her mistress.

Dublin was to become the centre for the slave trade for the Vikings in Ireland, with Bristol being an important exit port even then, well before the African slave trade centuries later. They probably also used Jorvik (York) and London as trading centres.

One could be born into slavery, although the Vikings had a rule about this: a child born to a free Viking and a slave woman was born free and classed as Norse (so long as his father admitted paternity), but children of a male Viking slave were destined to remain slaves. A slave injured in his master's service was entitled to medical care. A man could kill his slave, and if another person did it, they only had to make financial restitution. Vikings themselves sometimes became slaves of the Englisc: Edward the Elder brought back Viking slaves with his West Saxon & Mercian army.

A slave wishing to buy their freedom had to make two payments of silver. The second was at a ceremony called the frelsis oel (= free neck ale.) Ale was brewed containing three measures, making it as strong as 14% alcohol, and a sheep was slaughtered and eaten. This was sometimes termed logleiddr, meaning 'inducted into law', since a slave had no legal status. Once free, the ex-slave (leysingi) must not bring law-suits against his master or show disrespect. His former master still had a duty of care towards him if he fell upon hard times. The wergild (level of legal damages) for a freed slave was less than that of a free-born man and equivalent approximately to the price of a domestic animal.

There is the description by the Arab Ibn Fadlan of the slave girl ritually killed to accompany her dead master in his burning boat burial. This appears to have been a custom of Swedish Rus tribe traders operating on the River Volga and does not seem to have been reported elsewhere.

Norman Slavery

Whilst living in Normandy, France, the Normans (of Scandinavian descent) had slaves, brought mainly through the port of Rouen. After their conquest of England in 1066, there was a four pence tax per slave, payable to the king, but slavery was officially outlawed in England in 1102. After that, the trade continued elsewhere. In many ways the post - Norman conquest serfs were unofficial slaves - theoretically free but tied to one feudal overlord and piece of land and restricted from travel.

Portrait of a Sun God

Written for Gippeswic magazine

Idolised by his followers long after his death, many of whom believe he still lives on. On the various talismans, they accumulate he is pictured dressed in animal skins, and dancing in a drug-induced ecstasy to the shamanic drumming of his attendants. His yearly cycle between the Gracelands and the dark denizens of Sin City to the West confirm him in his role as a sun god.

Sun Records that is of course, for his name was Elvis Aaron Presley. Non-believers arguing it was merely a record company should take note that it was run by Sam ('Sun') Phillips, a blatant corruption of an earlier deity name. Elvis connects him to that dwarf worker of gold Alvis in the Northern mythology, and the latter part of his name (ley) to the sacred trackways of the heavens. His middle name Aaron though connects him with the lost tribes of Israel, which is proved by the name of his attendants, the Jordanaires. The Jews flight from Egypt is echoed in the rumours of his second coming on a complete CD Set, but conclusive confirmation is given when we find that his home was in Memphis. (This American city is the place that gave its name to the one in Egypt, and it is only a matter of time before the pyramids are excavated.) He also had a warrior aspect in later life, when he moved to RCA Victor records. His warlike deeds must have been quite notable, as a Colonel Tom Parker was merely his High Priest. His military exploits are contained within the ritual drama (i.e. it has no proper plot) *G.I. Blues.*

His spirit guide was thought to be a bear, from the evidence of the sacred chant "I just want to be your teddy bear", but some sources suggest he was more connected to a Hound Dog. What is certain, despite any exaggeration of his feats since death, is that he was originally a real person and not an idol. In one of the sacred texts, it states quite clearly "I don't have a wooden heart." Some recent research suggests that he expected to be cannibalised after death, but the translation of the "Love me tender" text remains controversial. Detractors from that school of thought cite his principal religious text "Don't be cruel" and believe that those of the cannibal persuasion will be condemned to a hell known as Heartbreak Hotel.

Something more mysterious is his role as a fertility figure. As one of the pantheon of lame god archetypes, he appears in many images as having a harelip, with animal skin coats (possibly white leather) embossed with rhinestones to signify the suns radiance. The significance of the turned-up collar is still to be explained, as have the blue suede shoes. It has also been suggested that the long, elaborate fringes on the coat represent solar flares. There are myths about him having flares around his feet as well, but this can never be proved due to the American TV taboo of never showing him below the waistline. What is known is that he had a female consort who later fell from grace called Priscilla.

Note 1. Sin City mentioned in paragraph one is also known as Las Vegas.
Note 2. The talismans mentioned in the same paragraph are frequently disguised as a bathmat.
I hope this bit of rubbish has given you a giggle. My apologies to any over-sensitive Presley fans. The point it makes though is that from twisting some words and unconnected facts together, you can seemingly 'prove' anything. The methods used and quality of so-called proof is of no lesser standard than I have seen from some writers, ley line hunters, TV documentaries and psychic questers.

A Heathen's attitude to illness and disability: a very personal view

As I get older, inevitably I experience the effects on my body in common with many others such as poorer eyesight, high blood pressure and arthritis. I also am an insulin-dependent diabetic and have had three incidences of cancer as well as depression. In that, I am no different to many other people. However, it has got me thinking about my attitude toward illness and disability.

Various other religions have distinct attitudes to illness: a punishment from a vengeful god, a deliberate trial to test one's faith or an opportunity to reach a spiritual enlightenment. However, Heathen beliefs are a little less clear. If we look at some Anglo- Saxon texts, we can see that some maladies were blamed upon 'elf-shot,' i.e. a supernatural intervention. Consequently, the remedies applied seem to have a magical element contained within them as well as practical herbal healing.

Within the Havamal, (Sayings of the High One) an Icelandic book of what appears to be a collection of proverbs we are told that a man that has lost a hand can still herd cattle.[1] It implies an

---

[1] Havamal stanza 71:

The halt can ride on horseback,
the one-handed drive cattle;
the deaf fight and be useful:

attitude of identifying what a disabled person can do, rather than what they cannot do, which is a common theme in modern social work thinking. It links in with the terminology that some healthcare organisations have adopted: 'differently-abled' instead of 'disabled.' One could scream 'political correctness' here, but I guess it is a way of changing attitudes by using differently constructed speech.

There does not appear to be any form of blaming a deity or other supernatural being for misfortune within Heathen mythology. However, one could possibly relate misfortune to the pre-determined orlög or hamingja of a person, which refers to an earned personal or family accrued 'luck.'

There is a Goddess of healing to appeal to though: Menglad or Eir. There are also healing rituals that involve an appeal to higher powers such as the Icelandic tale of Cormac where he is told to aid his recovery by sacrificing an ox at a mound where the Huldefolk dwell.

So, what is the modern Heathen to think about their illness or disability? Well, I think that it is generally agreed that our Germanic and Norse forefathers were very forward-thinking and embraced new technology. It would seem right then to seek whatever scientifically medical

---

to be blind is better
than to be burnt:
no one gets good from a corpse.

remedies are available. That doesn't, of course, preclude us from adopting more magical complementary medicines or even the shamanistic assistance of a volva or seidr worker to help the more accepted medical practices along. There is undoubtedly good historical evidence for using herbs in sources such as the Anglo Saxon Bald's Leech Book and the Norse Sagas.

We also have a Heathen ideal of trying to be independent and keeping a good reputation. That would seem to inform us that we should try to make the best of ourselves and not rely upon others, the government, the benefits system etc. any more than necessary. That may mean changing to a more suitable occupation like the man who has lost a hand. It would certainly imply adopting a stoic attitude and not complaining about our condition but getting on with life the best we can.

That leads on to how Heathens regard others who have illness or disabilities: are we concerned for them, do we try to help them practically and spiritually? Do we treat them as equals who just happen to have a particular problem? I would like to think that we adopt the positive attitudes shown towards Paralympic athletes in the last few years. We may even link a mythological story to reality: the deliberately lamed blacksmith Wayland Smith[2] has parallels in other cultural mythologies, demonstrating a lamed god/ person overcoming adversity.

What is our attitude to 'sending healing' in the way that our counterparts in the general Pagan community do? Of course, that is dependent on a personal belief that (a) magic exists and (b) you can do it, something that I know some fellow Heathens would take issue with. My position is that I do send healing runes, etc., so long as they are requested: however, I do not believe in doing magic for people without them knowing, requesting or consenting to it. After all, in the broader world of the Wyrd, their illness or injury may be preventing them taking a potentially much more damaging action or decision, so they should take personal responsibility for any action taken on their behalf.

Summing up in my own life, I will remain belligerent and bloody-minded towards my illnesses and feel fully justified in sending a powerful curse upon any cancer that dares to have the temerity to assault me. I will not allow arthritis, diabetes, depression or whatever else Loki can throw at me to prevent me enjoying life and doing the things I want to do, from working and re-enacting to writing and lecturing. I will try to recognise that a spark of the gods and goddesses are within everyone, (however hard that is to find) meaning that I should value

[2] See 'Blacksmith Gods'

everyone regardless of whether I like them or not. I will inevitably fail because I am an imperfect human, but I will keep on grumpily trying.

A revision of personality types.

After extensive reading and research, I have become aware that many people apply inaccurate personal descriptive words. As a benefit to society, I would like to share a few of my own updated definitions from the forthcoming book Jennings, Pete (2027) *Why I am right*. (Published in a hardback firm enough to hit people over the head with.)

Plucky: a term used to describe a person too thick to know when they are beaten. He faces unbeatable odds while his comrades run and hide. When taken for execution, he sticks tongue out and blows raspberry just before the axe falls. *Plucky* should not be confused with *Lucky*: in that case, the axeman executioner would miss and chop his own foot off, and the chap would escape in the confusion.

Adventurous: a person who when it is suggested that they have sex with a tiger asks, 'what could possibly go wrong?'

Humorous: the quality of seeing the lighter side of any situation, including death, zombie apocalypse, and visiting Basildon.

Gregarious: the tendency of someone to be obnoxiously cheerful and friendly to all and sundry, regardless of their situation or character. He would have probably made friends with Hitler if only he could have got into the bunker but wasted too much time trying out 'knock -knock' jokes with the guards.

Knowledgeable: the quality of being a smart arse without reference to Google or Wikipedia. Can lecture for hours (and does) on obscure subjects of no interest to the majority of people (the history of cornflakes for example) but utterly devoid of any practical advice such as how to mend a car, hide a body or invade Poland.

Reclusive: pathologically allergic to fresh air, sunshine, people and modern life. Their best friend is a library. When they die, they will not be discovered until their cats have half-eaten their corpse.

Eccentric: people who are not normal like me. They listen to boring crap bands, wear bland clothes and watch rubbish TV programmes.

After the Abyss, Ginnugagap.

A poem initially published in Gippeswic magazine.

Sometimes I get close to the edge.
It's frightening, half seeing
Things out of the corner of your eye
And knowing if you turn they'll disappear.
I strove for this situation
And am pleased that I have achieved it,
But it is a two-edged weapon;
The one to cut away the old,
The other to thrust for the new.
No one can tell you what to expect
When you face the Abyss.
Alone, naked and frightened
Your worst nightmares come to life,
Tailor-made to your own darkest recesses.
All the preparations you made are never enough
And you need every bit of hard-won knowledge
Plus the other skills
Learnt as you experience them
To even survive, let alone retain your sanity.

On returning, elated, exhausted
One sees with different eyes.
Experience with different, heightened senses.
For a period it is hard to control,
And some poor souls never manage it,
To be locked away
With what others call delusions.

Once it was mainly a mainly mundane life you
led
With odd glimpses of that other world.
Now that world is more real than this
And it is hard to cope,
To not permanently drift away,
Whilst going through the mechanical motions
Of this everyday existence.

The Universal Psychic Reading

I used to sometimes work as a reader of runes and tarot. Inevitably, the different readers at psychic fairs got to know each other and laughed about some of the less scrupulous colleagues who would milk the client for information, then feed it back to them in startlingly accurate readings! More amusing still were those who had a series of phrases they trotted out which the client would always identify with (from Adolf Hitler to Mother Theresa) and would fit what 99% of the worlds' population thinks about itself. From overhearing quite a few of these between us, we came up with a collective 'ultimate suits all, one size fits everyone, stunningly accurate' reading. It went something like this:

'Ah, there you are! I knew you would eventually come – you have been debating it with yourself to have a reading for some time, haven't you? Of course, you could be this side of the table yourself. You are quite psychic, aren't you, but you seem to be a little nervous about using it? I see you at a crossroads in your life. Things could go either way you know, but you must listen to your heart. The trouble is you let people impose upon your good nature. They take advantage of you, don't they? It is a pity they don't have a bit more sensitivity for your feelings – deep down, you are a very sensitive, caring person.

Money is a bit of a struggle, isn't it? All I can say is that as you sow so shall you reap. I am afraid I cannot see you having any major windfall from a lottery win though, and of course, work never brings in a reward of what you are worth. Somebody seems to block your way there, ' although they never make it obvious, and may pretend to be your friend. It is such a pity because I can see what an ethical, fair-minded person you are.

I see a minor ailment coming sometime, but it is nothing out of the ordinary, so do not worry yourself about it. I should watch how you lift heavy things though – get somebody else to help you. Home life continues much the same – I can see you have excellent taste in the things you surround yourself with. By the way – you are going to read or hear something very interesting to you soon!

Growing up was hard for you. Other children can be so cruel and fickle. And you have known the sorrow of somebody you knew dying. They speak from the other side and tell me to say they are alright now. The romance seems to have gone out of life around you, but you will always be a survivor until the day you die, which should be a long way off (excluding accidents!)' Some of this reading may not make much sense to you at the moment, but it will do eventually, just you see. Or to someone you know quite well.

THE SAXON SAINT OF MARCH

Written for Ða Engliscan Gesiðas (The English Companions) Wiðowinde (Bindweed) magazine.

I spent the first part of 2016 working in the Fenland town of March, and each day passed a handsome church, much later than the Anglo-Saxon period but dedicated to Wendreda. It is the only dedication made to her to my knowledge, but she is the patron saint of the town. I am told that there were originally two Saxon settlements on the old course of the River Nene, Merche (OE Mearc = boundary) and Merchford, at the fording place on the river. [3]

The church itself is of a much later date but was built over the original Anglo-Saxon shrine. The Normans came and rebuilt in stone, leaving a massive stone font with incised geometric patterns on the sides. Later the church was re-modelled again, and the corners of the font were taken off to fit in with the new pillars. The church has the largest Church Bible in use anywhere and a walkway under part of the church tower so as not to interfere with an existing footpath. There are two 'squints' in the tunnel that allegedly allowed lepers to look into the church without infecting healthy parishioners!

[3] Pollington (1993) gives two other words for boundary: gemære and londgemære.

However, what most visitors notice first are the 120 carved wooden angels in the double hammer beamed roof, carved from oak at Bacton, Suffolk and transported there in 1526. To make sure that they do not make the church completely perfect (reserved for the Christian God) a crude devil's face is carved into one of the supports. However, there are some other figures around, and towards the back of the church is a carved wooden figure of Wendreda herself. Her image is also repeated in a modern stained-glass window and banner.

I was already familiar with the name of Wendreda, as a side note to my research into King Onna (or Anna) of the East Anglian Wuffing dynasty. King Penda of Mercia had forced Onna into exile after the Battle of Cnobheresburh in about 651 CE, which is generally believed to be the old monastery and Roman fort at Burgh on the Suffolk / Norfolk border. (Jennings, 2013) After Onna returned, he died at or soon after the battle of Bulcamp in about 653-4 (to the east of Blyford, on the opposite side of the estuary to Blythburgh, Suffolk)[4] fighting Penda. His son Eormen (also identified as St. Jurmin of Beodricsworth) died in the battle. Apart from territorial ambitions, it is likely that Penda was particularly against Onna for sheltering the exiled

---

[4] Coincidentally, the massive church at Blythbugh like March and Woolpit also has masses of carved angels in its roof.

Cenwalh, the King of Wessex who had abandoned Penda's sister.

The Anglo-Saxon Chronicle says that Botwulf (St. Botolph) founded a minster at Icanhoh (Iken) not far away in Suffolk, which may have been to commemorate Onna. That wonderful little church (later raided by Vikings in 870) on the river Alde still has a four-and-a-half-foot fragment of an Anglo-Saxon stone cross within it, with a dragon, cross and interlace pattern.

Although the King Raedwald (died c.625 CE) had his palace at Rendlesham not far from the royal cemetery at Sutton Hoo, his indirect descendant Onna was recorded as living at Exning near Newmarket. Whether he used Rendlesham as well is not known. Still, it may be that he wanted to be closer to the defensive Devils Dyke ditches that partly protected East Anglia from the north by continuing the barrier of the Wash and the marshy Fens, which extended much further inland at that time.

What we do know is that at least one of his daughters was born at Exning. King Onna (who was much influenced by St. Felix of Burgundy) left four daughters who became acknowledged as saints: Æðeldryð (sometimes referred to as Ethelreda) was born in Exning in 630 and married Tondberht, ealdorman of the South Gyrwas in the Fens. On his death in 655 she went into a nunnery at Cratendune near Ely but was not to be left in contemplation for more than five years. In 660 she was married to the 15-year-old Ecgfriđ who became King of Northumbria, as a way of Oswiu consolidating power in a Northumbrian – East Anglian alliance against the power of Mercia. However, Bishop Wilfred later encouraged her to enter the Northumbrian monastery at Coldingham. She had dissolved her marriage to the much younger king (who had an alternative partner Eormenburga in mind.) From Coldingham, she later returned to her East Anglian roots to found an Abbey at Ely. (Thomas of Ely, c.1174)

Æđeldryđ's three sisters were Seaxburh (improbably, also known as Seaxburga!), Æđelburh (Ethelburga) and Wihtburh (Withburga). They also all went on to have noted lives:

Seaxburh married King Eorcenberht of Kent and founded a monastery at Sheppey. After her husband's death, she went to be an Abbess at her sister's foundation at Ely. Æđelburh went to a double monastery in Northern France called Faremoutiers-en-Brie, which was run by her stepsister by her mother's previous husband, Seđryd. She eventually took over as Abbess herself. Wihtburh founded a Nunnery at Dereham, Norfolk and a well in the churchyard is named after her. As a saint, her bones were later moved to Ely.

So where does Wendreda come in?[5] There have been thoughts in the past that her name is a corruption of Æðelðryð, but their stories are very different. It is possible that she was another younger daughter, not recorded at the same time as the others. Alternatively, she was a high-born woman of Onna's court but not directly related to him as a daughter. There is a St. Wendreda's Well in Exning, one of a set of springs where she is said to have practised healing. I understand that it is now in the private grounds of the Hamilton Stud. One needs to seek permission from the owners to visit it. (OS TL 621645)

Wendreda moved to the March area where she continued healing both people of the Gyrwas tribal group and their animals. She may have been influenced by the missionary Felix or the other ladies from Onna's court. Other Christians were working or becoming hermits in the Fens, such as Saints Guthlac and Etheldrifa, at Croyland, St. Pega of Peakirk and St Huna of Chatteris. She would have plenty to keep her occupied, as it was a wet area associated with malaria and cholera. There is also a tradition of a nunnery sited close to the church, but no current evidence is available. When she died, the popular woman was given a costly funeral and burial. Her feast day is January 22nd. The

[5] Wendreda inevitably is given some alternative names: Saint Wyndred the Virgin (Gild certificate of 1389) Wendrille & Wendreth (Liber Eliensis 2)

church guidebook (Bevis, 2013) provides a version of what happened next. Abbot Aelfsige (or Aelsi) got permission to remove her body to Ely. However, in 1016 her remains were taken by monks to Edmund Ironside.

The idea was to carry the relics at the head of an Englisc army against the Danes: when I say it was the Battle of Assundon (Ashingdon) in Essex, one could expect for them to be lost. However, despite the disastrous Saxon defeat their Danish conqueror King Cnut was said to have been converted to Christianity by their story and presence on the battlefield and passed them onto Canterbury Cathedral. Somehow through this Wendreda was seen as a peacemaker, and a symbol of two doves became associated with her. In about 1343 her remains were returned to the restored church at March. They stayed as the centre of pilgrimage and a Gild altar until about 1545 when the Reformation removed most of such items. Whether the relic was hidden or destroyed then is not known. However, in 2011 the Cambridge Times reported:

HISTORIAN Trevor Bevis has rung the bells at St Wendreda's in March for 64 years - but one slice of the ancient church's history has always troubled him. Now, after years of study, the 81-year-old believes he has finally discovered the burial site of St Wendreda's relic - just inches beneath the church floor. Overlooked by a stained-glass window of the saint herself, in the south aisle of the church, a stone slab is marked with a faint 'S' - thought to represent either saint or Sanctus - and a tell-tale strip of copper.

(Cambs Times 27 August 2011)

References

Bevis T. (2005) Wendreda the Peacemaker. March

Bevis, T. (2013) The story of a famous Fen Church: Saint Wendreda, March. March

Jennings, P. (2013) Penda, Heathen King of Mercia: his Anglo-Saxon world. Halstead: Gruff Books.

Pollington, S. (1993) Wordcraft Pinner: Anglo Saxon Books

Smith, A. (1994) Sixty Saxon Saints. Hockwold-cum-Wilton: Anglo Saxon Books

Thomas of Ely. (c.1174) Liber Eliensis (Book of Ely) Ely. [Translated in Fairweather, J.(trans.), ed. (2005). Liber Eliensis. Woodbridge, UK: Boydell Press

Suffolk Mountain Rescue Team – Summit to think about.

The report[6] in 2009 that Gt. Britain was tilting (Scotland gaining altitude, Southern England losing it) plus the wetter, muddier conditions brought about by global warming have increased the chances of mountains sliding southwards across Gt Britain. Concerned about the possible effect that this new phenomenon may have upon the flatlands of East Anglia, pioneering volunteers have formed the Suffolk Mountain Rescue Team. Team Leader Pete Jennings explained that they would aim to rescue any mountains that have broken loose and help them to relocate in the hillier parts of the South Coast where they will be much more at home. "The idea is to give them a helping push on their way. We are also negotiating with British Rail Freight to set up a '7 Day Mountain Pass' ticket to keep them off the roads."

"We will, of course, rescue any walkers, rock climbers or mountaineers who are feeling peaky trapped on them as well" Pete Jennings added. "Already the National Trust has allowed us to use Mound 2 at Sutton Hoo for abseiling training in the absence of any other hills in Suffolk, assisted by the French expert Madame Ava

6
http://www.telegraph.co.uk/news/earth/earthnews/6226537/England-is-sinking-while-Scotland-rises-above-sea-levels-according-to-new-study.html

L'Anche. Meanwhile, we are making a modest start: veteran Gran Ite and her team are repatriating rocks brought home by holiday makers back into their natural habitat by returning them by post in protective jiffy bags. It starts with the odd pebble, but we have seen them get a little boulder recently."

"Suffolk Mountain Rescue Team is available 24/7 except for Ipswich Town home games. We have had a few false alarms but better that than to ignore genuine cases." The team were recently spotted in their distinctive high-altitude bobble hats, roped together on a window ledge in Christchurch Park. It turned out that a council workman was making mountains out of mole hills, but the team have been successful in rescuing a Suffolk couple suffering from altitude sickness on Bent Hill, Felixstowe.

Chief Fundraiser Cliff Fall is appealing for donations of more jiffy bags and postage stamps at the teams Alpe Street HQ in Ipswich, a stone's throw from Norwich Road. There, a retired vet is training mountain goats in rescuing. "They are much better at climbing than rescue dogs," said Al Pine, "and better also at carrying the small kegs of Adnams beer around their necks."

Critics have attacked Norfolk for not taking the situation seriously. "They are just sticking their heads in the Yarmouth sand are hoping that any incoming mountains will fall into the sea like their eroding coastline," said an irate activist Mr I. Plummet (62). "I hope that people from around the country will add their support to the Suffolk Mountain Rescue Team. They can take the plunge and join them for free by 'liking' this article on Cliff Facebook."

A benefit rock concert is being held to fund the team with headliners the Rolling Stones and Dave Edmund's Rockpile. However, an un-named spokesperson for the English Defence League threatened they would picket it: "These migrant mountains are coming down here and taking the jobs of hard-working English Pennines" they said. "Some of them are also terrorists: we have already heard of a big one called Osama Ben Nevis."

Meanwhile, the East Anglian Tourist Board refused to comment on rumours that they have applied for outline planning permission to build a funicular railway, ski lodges and cable car system at an undisclosed location in Suffolk.

A Heathen temple nearly missed?

Published initially in Wiðowinde, the Journal of The English Companions (Ða Engliscan Gesiðas)

I have been working in Harlow, Essex recently and made some time to check out the temple site. I had heard it referred to as a Roman Temple but found that it was, in fact, the location of four distinct religious phases: Bronze Age, Celtic, Roman and Anglo Saxon. It is a scheduled ancient monument, tucked away in the corner of an industrial estate.

A Bronze Age barrow of about 2000BCE was the first known structure, but in around 100BCE a Celtic temple site was constructed there. The invading Romans put their distinct mark on the site when in about 80CE they built a square *'cella'* temple with a surrounding wooden palisade. Later around 100-120CE, the palisade was replaced with stone walls, two cobbled courtyards and two side rooms. The outlines (picked out in modern paving slabs) and the raised rectangular mound can still be seen there today if you brave the slightly overgrown footpath to it.[7]

---

[7] Take the A414 route through Harlow. Where it becomes the Edinburgh Way turn off at the roundabout onto River Way. On the industrial site, opposite the Pitney Bowes factory you will see a piece of rough ground to your right, with a much faded 'Roman Temple' sign. Follow the footpath (which had chest high nettles when I visited) until you find the information boards. The temple

This Roman temple continued to be used until the later part of the 4th century when it fell into disrepair. It is possible that the Romano British in the area converted to Christianity or some other religion then. There were plenty of alternative Roman and Celtic deities some of which were worshipped dualistically such as the local goddess (Celtic) Sulis Minerva (Roman) at Bath. The Harlow temple is believed to have been dedicated to Minerva from a limestone statue head found there. Finds listed on the website are all dated between 43AD to 400AD of the Romano British period before the Angles, Jutes & Saxons generally settled in England.[8]

According to the public information display boards around the site[9], in around 500CE the Anglo Saxons created a Pagan temple on the same location. It is shown on the maps as an area towards the eastern corner of the Roman courtyard. Sometimes Heathen temples are known as *hearg* (harrow), but these are arguably outdoor religious sites, and give us some place

---

site is a raised rectangular mound marked out with paving slabs.

[8]
http://unlockingessex.essexcc.gov.uk/content_page.asp?content_page_id=120&content_parents=48,94

[9] Timeline on these are given as: 5000 BC Mesolithic Hunter Gatherer Encampment, 2000 BC Bronze Age Pond Barrow, 200 BC Celtic Temple built, AD 80 Roman Temple built, AD 200 Temple rebuilt, AD 375-400 Temple destroyed, AD 500 Saxon Temple built, AD 600 Site finally abandoned

names such as Harrow on the Hill, Sussex) and Harrow Fields, Cheshire.[10]

It wasn't just Christians who re-used previous religious sites! According to the information boards, the Anglo- Saxon area seems to have been used for a hundred years or more, which would take us up to the time of Christian conversion again in the early 7th century. There is no indication of what form the Anglo-Saxon temple took from the archaeologists than explored the site in the 1960s and 1980s. Still, they are generally believed elsewhere to be rectangular.[11] Finds from the site are said to be held mainly held in the Harlow Museum, yet when I visited there were just three Anglo Saxon brooches on display, none of which were from this site.

Maybe the pottery shards are stored away as not of much public interest. Inevitably there is a sizeable section on the Romans. It has been noticed before that the *Englisc* often seem to create their cemeteries or mounds near to earlier ones.

---

[10] Semple, S. (2007). *Defining the OE Hearg: A preliminary archaeological and topographic examination of hearg place names and their hinterlands.* Early Medieval Europe 15 (4): 364-385.

[11] Blair, J. (1995) *Anglo-Saxon pagan shrines and their prototypes.* Anglo-Saxon Studies in Archaeology and History 8: 1-28.

One could almost be forgiven for thinking that the Anglo-Saxon component of the site was non-existent if one simply read the report of the West Essex Archaeological group who excavated 1962-71. They concluded that the Romano-British temple *'was the last stage in a long religious development of the site.'* [12] Yet the Historic Environment Assessment of 2013 says *"The temple precinct was destroyed by fire and systematically dismantled in the late fourth century. There is some indication of continued use of the ruins, as evidenced by a hearth and associated stake-holes found within one of the small rooms flanking the temple entrance, and a timber structure abutting the outside wall."*

One wonders who was have supposed to have done this? The Romans had gone, so it either had to be some surviving Celtic Britons or some arriving Anglo Saxons. The notes of Richard Bartlett who excavated in the 1980s were not published, in part due to his premature death. However, they have now been digitised and can be read online.[13] In a report, he noted *POST*

---

[12] P.137 of Clark & Gobel (1985) *The Romano-British Temple at Harlow*. West Essex Archaeological Group: Gloucester.

[13]

http://archaeologydataservice.ac.uk/archives/view/harlow_hm_20 16/ includes descriptions of two 5-7th century Anglo Saxon brooches found at nearby Pishiobury Lock on the River Stort. One is an equal armed cross in copper / tin alloy, the other a cruciform long brooch. (Detailed in a 2016 report digitised from the Bartlett Excavation Archive.)

ROMAN ACTIVITY: The later history of the site has been confused by the 1972 landscaping. A single sherd of middle Saxon pottery was recovered from the disturbed former ground surface. However, the nature of the landscaping has undoubtedly removed important evidence for any post-Roman activity that may have existed on the site.[14]

Maybe this explains the lack of material in Harlow museum if it was limited to a single pottery shard. One could ask why anyone should deduce that an Anglo-Saxon religious site existed if only a single pottery shard were found? (Particularly as it was said to be Mid-Saxon, by when the populace was at least officially Christian.) It could just as well be something accidentally dropped or moved during the 1972 landscaping mentioned above. However, Baker[15] says that there was a *'large amount of 5-7th century pottery has been recovered from the site as well as three early Anglo-Saxon brooches.'* Who are we to believe? He also mentions that the remains of an *'earth fast timber structure was recognised above the Roman destruction layer.'* Further research reveals that the eastern sector of the site was the last to be excavated, which

[14] Bartlett, R. (1986) *Harlow Temple Excavations 1985-86 An Interim Report*

[15] Baker, J.T. (2005) *Cultural Transition in the Chilterns and Essex Region, 350AD – 650AD. Studies in Regional and Local History Vol. 4.* Univ. of Hertfordshire Press: Hertfordshire

may explain the more substantial Anglo Saxon remains only being reported then. One wonders somewhat cynically though if the earlier excavators were so intent on revealing the Roman remains that they missed the evidence nearer the surface or misinterpreted it through not expecting to find it?

Descriptions of Norse Viking temples in Iceland[16] and elsewhere sometimes include a semi-circular apse at one end in which statues of deities are placed and a stand for the symbolic arm ring of the priest or priestess (*Goði & Gyða*) used for taking oaths. However, we know that there are at least some differences between Norse and Anglo- Saxon practice: unlike the Saxon Coifi Icelandic priests were allowed to bear arms and ride a stallion.[17] There was, however, the same prohibition on taking weapons into the Vé sacred space.

So, from an Anglo- Saxon perspective, is Harlow temple site much to get worked up about? My answer to that is yes; we know of very few such sites other than those later colonised by the Christian church. We have Bede's[18] description

---

[16] Jennings, P. (2007) *Heathen Paths: Viking & Anglo Saxon Pagan Beliefs*. Capall Bann: Milverton.

[17] The Goði Hrafnkel in the *Saga of Hrafnkel* (Gunnell, 1997)

[18] Bede (1951) *Historia Ecclesiastica The Ecclesiastical history of the English Nation* Dent & Sons: London

of Rædwald's temple at Rendlesham Suffolk (with its twin altars of Pagan and Christian gods) and now that the settlement has been excavated maybe even the site, if it is not under St. Gregory's Church.

We also know from Bede that there was a Pagan temple at Goodmanham in Yorkshire where the turncoat Pagan high priest Coifi[19] threw a spear in 627 CE to demonstrate a change of faith to Christianity in conjunction with king Edwin of Northumbria. He was breaking taboos about his role: riding a stallion, bearing weapons and taking a weapon into the temple and finally setting fire to it. It is thought to lie under or near All Hallows Church, formerly an Anglo- Saxon wooden structure replaced in about 1130CE by the later stone Anglo-Norman church seen today. That is so often the case. After all, Pope Gregory wrote to Abbot Mellitus in instructing him to convert Pagan shrines into Christian sites since so many of them were well made, and the result would be only one choice of place to worship.[20]

---

[19] Pollington discusses theories that Coifi may not be the actual name of the priest: it seems to be an Anglicisation of a Brythonic name or a term for a priest indicating that he was hooded. Pollington, S. (2011) *The Elder Gods.* Anglo Saxon Press: Little Downham.

[20] Foster, S. *Religion and the Landscape – How the conversion affected the Anglo-Saxon landscape and its role in Anglo-Saxon ideology.* The School of Historical Studies Postgraduate Forum. University of Newcastle E-Journal Edition 6, 2007/08

There are of course some place names associated with Old English gods such as Wansdyke, Wednesbury (Woden's Barrow) Wednesfield (Woden's field), Thundersley (þunor's grove), Thurstable (þunor's pillar), and Tysoe (Tiw's Hill Spur) etc. However, these names only give the area of a cult, not the specific site, although they do provide some indication of regional variations in which gods were acknowledged. There are also some Pagan period Anglo Saxon cemeteries with traces of rectangular wooden buildings in them, such as at Lyminge, Kent. Whether they were of purely practical use or had a ceremonial aspect cannot be known at present.

The well- known 7th century Anglo Saxon royal settlement at Yeavering, Northumberland does have a reasonable contender for a Pagan temple: building D2 had an extensive collection of ox skulls associated with it. (Funnily enough, I heard about one Methodist chapel in the Fens that had ox skulls deposited at each corner of its foundations which were discovered during later building work!) Whether the ox skulls were simply the remains of religious feasting, sacrifice or had some other meaning is open to conjecture. Five hundred metres to the South of the Harlow temple site is the Saxon settlement of

[21] Essex County Council (2013) *Templefields LDO - Historic Environment Assessment.* Essex County Council: Chelmsford

Harlowbury.[21] The name of Harlow itself has been interpreted as either deriving from Old English words 'here' and 'hlaw', meaning 'army hill' or alternatively 'here' and 'hearg', meaning 'temple hill' which given the subject of this article I naturally prefer.

Given the religious nature of the Anglo Saxons, before and after conversion we seem to have a dearth of undiscovered Heathen temples in England. Even if some have not been identified separately from other buildings, it would seem natural that each of the many separate kingdoms that existed before 630CE would have had a more significant centralised 'royal' temple for local kings and their followers to worship in. Undoubtedly many will be underneath the foundations of later Christian churches, which mean that we should always stay alert to any excavations.

Marine Ritual

Written initially for Pagan Humour (2005)

It has been realised that Paganism will never achieve popular status with its' current forms. Therefore, it has been decided that a new form of authorised observance will be created that will seek to be sympathetic to the needs of the average British couple. The ideal time for newcomers to be introduced to the craft is when they are relaxed and close to nature, so what better time than on a seaside holiday?

The priest shall wear a knotted hanky on his head, with trousers rolled up to the knees. (This is symbolic of the Masonic iconography and the four knots the elemental directions.) The priestess shall wear a swimsuit one size too small, a kiss me quick hat (representing the sexuality of the Goddess) and an optional plastic mac. They will create a sacred space by spreading two beach towels (except in Germany where this is taboo before 5 am.) This may be augmented by a ring of sand pies. A Blackpool Watchtower will be erected at each quarter, starting in the East and working in the same direction as the roller coaster. The elements will then be invoked. (This is particularly easy at English holiday resorts, sometimes known as last resorts. The plastic mac may be useful here.) To make participants feel at home, familiar seaside objects should be used to represent the four elements: We suggest a whoopee cushion for air, a Calor gas stove for fire, a leaking plastic sand pie bucket for water and a sandcastle for earth.

Once the sacred space has been created, further rituals such as anointing each other with the holy ointment (Ambre Solaire), and the reading of the Sunday newspaper can be performed. (On reaching the section on naughty vicars the sacred Egyptian banishing mantra of 'Tut Tut' may be intoned.) A warm Coke and a stale Steak and Kidney pie may be substituted for the more usual cakes and ale, and 'Sod that wasp' replace 'Blessed Be' as the most used response.

Editor's note: Due to the inability of the Pagan writer of this piece to relate to what is happening in the real world, he was unaware that similar rituals to this have already been celebrated for many years.

A personal reflection of the Heathen Gods in my life.

Until my early teens, I was an active member of the Church of England, so I guess I have always had a spiritual life of one form or another. One of the main reasons I left in the early seventies was that it seemed to have 'something missing' and I ended up disagreeing with more than I could agree. Briefly, I had a Roman Catholic girlfriend and was persuaded to visit her church. I felt that their acknowledgement of Mary as a feminine divine figure was maybe part of the 'something missing', but I did not like much of the rest of their doctrine, and it didn't seem that their devotion to Mary was reflected in their attitude to women.

Spiritually I drifted for a bit and got married to someone against all religion, but still read quite extensively until I found Paganism as a path more reflecting my feelings about divinity. In particular, I was attracted to Heathenry (then termed Odinism). By the time I divorced in the late eighties, I knew which organisations I wanted to join to catch up with the practical aspects that I had only read about until then. Inevitably I met a lot of Pagans of other paths as well.

Some seemed only to be concerned with a Goddess. I could appreciate that after millennia of subjugation by men that women may want to redress the balance. It seemed to me that some of them had gone too far the other way: as the former oppressed, shouldn't they know not to do the same thing the other way around? I wanted more balance than that, and my self-awareness developed as a psychotherapist informed me that we all have elements of both genders within us, physically, psychologically and emotionally.

I did not want to be a male second-class Goddess worshipper or a Wiccan. Neither did I seek to join the ranks of what I saw as the 'Iron John' or 'Merlin Quest' [22] counter-reaction movement by males feeling rejected by feminists and only relating to a group of macho Gods. I can understand a group of men or women deciding to work exclusively together but feel then that there is even more of a need for a counter balancing divinity of the opposite gender, especially if one has feelings of balancing polarity or divine partnership. A group of men or group of women can acknowledge a god and goddess without compromising their masculinity or femininity. This must be especially evident now in a time when we have male midwives, female engineers and traditional gender stereotypes are challenged daily.

[22]   Iron John: A Book About Men is a book by American poet Robert Bly published in 1990 by Addison-Wesley.

The Merlin Quest is based upon the various writings and teachings of RJ Stewart

Since working for the Pagan Federation, (eventually as President) I have continued to be involved with Pagans of many different spiritual paths. My learning about their many ways and experiences lead to the writing of 'Pagan Paths' which details the differences and similarities between the groupings available to European Pagans in 2002. I continue to find the interchange of differing views enlightening and stimulating to my faith.

Heathenism became the ideal for me. The Old Norse texts spoke of there being an equal number of Gods and Goddesses, although in those early days of the 1970s and 1980s there were far more males into the path and adopting Odin as their chief deity. I followed suit at the time but made sure of also exploring the Goddesses such as Freyja, Frigga and Holda as well. Most non-Heathens fail to recognise that despite Odin (or Anglo Saxon Woden) being named as the chief God, most of the ordinary people in the past paid more attention to Thor (Thunor.) As a God of fertility and defender against hostile forces, he was far more critical than one who was more aligned with leadership, politics and esoteric magic.

It is strange in some ways that the Viking peoples, renowned for their love of being true to your word, defending your kin and respecting the family should have a God Odin. Within the mythology, he seems to deceive others frequently, switches sides on a whim and seduces any attractive female he finds. Yet don't all people tend to shape their gods as images of themselves, and sometimes get the god they deserve? He teaches me how power can be misused and how he had to make many sacrifices for the wisdom he gained. E.g. his eye for the knowledge of Mimir's well, hanging for nine days and nights from the world tree Yggdrasill, pierced by his spear to gain the knowledge of the runes which he seizes from the primal void Ginnugagap. In winning the understanding of the Vanir Seidr magic from Freyja, Odin even gains a reputation for being effeminate, a dreadful accusation within that historical period of Norse culture. It is yet another message to modern heterosexual Heathens such as me: you may have to let go of everything, including your gender stereotypes to become as one with the gods, and to accept that others may have to do so. I have no place for homophobic or racist beliefs within what I define as my version of Heathenry, and I think the fact that there are some prominent gay and lesbian individuals within modern Heathenism, (as well as a more significant female presence) is evidence of how the movement has developed and embraced contemporary attitudes. My researches and personal opinions about the path are mainly contained in my book 'Heathen Paths.'

Eventually, as my life changed in many ways, I came to appreciate Thor / Thunor more. He has a reputation for hitting first and asking questions afterwards, a much more direct and simplistic approach than the craftier Odin. I regret that I resemble Thors image in many ways! I retain my ability to work craftily (the advantage of more than sixty years of life experience) yet tend now to be more confrontational and take on what I see as unfairness much more directly. Diplomacy was never my strong suit anyway, so hopefully, it causes me less stress as I become more intolerant with ageing. In openly challenging what I see as wrong, I am also in touch with the trickster God Loki. Although he is often seen as evil, he is sometimes the only one that dares to tell the truth, as in the Flyting of Loki myth, where he exposes the wrong doings of the other deities at a feast. His is a two-edged ability though, and he eventually oversteps the mark in being responsible for the death of Balder, for which he is punished. It is interesting to compare his identity with the Christian devils: The name Satan does not translate as evil, but 'Opposer' or 'Questioner' and Lucifer as 'Light bringer'. The Trickster god is important in many cultures, as is the lesson of how far one should go to entertain, and how far is 'too far.'

With over one hundred deities, the North European Germanic pantheon has many gods and goddesses from which to choose. Frey is another popular one, but there are many others, such as the heroic Tyr and the God of Judgement Forseti that I can relate to. I also have an interest in gods of specific attributes, including the Völundr / Wayland Smith mythology that leads me to research and write 'Blacksmith Gods' book with material from many cultures and traditions. As someone with a background in folk music and traditions the cross over between folklore and mythology is a fertile area for me and so similarly, I wrote 'The Wild Hunt and its followers' and 'Old Glory & the Cutty Wren.' In writing such books, I am exploring my spirituality while sharing my researches with others and realising that they may view and utilise the material I present in ways very different from my own.

Although agreeing to visualise Thor as a red-bearded chap with a hammer is a handy shorthand way of communicating, I tend to personally think of the deities as archetypes of aspects of my own higher self rather than picturesque exterior beings. This is probably a product of my psychological training. It leads me back to my need for balance: Pagans may often say that the God or Goddess 'dwells within everyone' even if they are hard to see, and for that reason, we should regard everyone else in that way, however objectionable they appear to be. I find that quite a hard concept to deal with sometimes but believe that it is essentially true.

It also means that I have to have some Goddesses in my life, and Freyja, Frigga and Holda have a special meaning for me, and I try to acknowledge them regularly as well, albeit not always as much as my gods. I think the move to recognise and be influenced by a multitude of gods and goddesses has very much benefitted the modern Heathen community and made it more attractive to both women and the general Pagan community as a whole. I can acknowledge how Heathenism has developed differently and is perceived in some other countries (not always for the better.) From its' position of an isolated minority within the general Pagan community in the 1970s, it has grown numerically and spiritually to become a very vocal, popular and essential part of the diversity of the modern UK Pagan world.

The Rite of the Roll

Written for Gippeswic magazine.

The roll should be gathered at the appropriate time and place, i.e. any superstore opening on Sunday, and should be of the genus, *Lyons Choclatus Swiss.* This is of some importance as the name implies its origins within the mythical kingdom of Lyonesse. They are often found together in a box of the mystical number 2X3=6 (or did until the Chaos boys got at it.)

Place the roll in a circle, (I suggest a dinner plate) and call it into being with the following invocation: (Lay upon the floor and yodel loudly.) When you have summoned sufficient power, turn over, and if successful you will have performed the Rite of the Swiss Roll, as perfected by Frater Plonkermus.

Now open the silver foil and gaze within its depth. A likeness of the deity within yourself will be reflected. Examine the contents, and the chocolate covering may be removed to reveal the sacred mystery of the Dark and Light forces spiralling together. Is the spiral inward or outward flowing? This has an inter-connectedness with the starlore of the Ancients concerning the Spiral Nebula. You may also notice a slight flattening at the bottom, connecting it to the Rollright Stone Circle in Oxfordshire.

The object is obviously a phallic symbol, as can be seen from its shape, and the way it ejaculates a creamy substance from one end. Some folklorists argue that this is the original form of the Maypole. One should always consume the swiss roll from the deosil spiral end to avoid creating negative energies.

Finally, do not forget to offer a portion back to the Goddess. The usual sequence is crumbs onto jumper, to be returned to the Earth via the washing machine drain pipe.

THE WILD HUNT & IT'S FOLLOWERS

The following work was issued as a small booklet in 2013 but has been out of print for some time.

INTRODUCTION

I became interested in aspects of the Wild Hunt long ago in my teens. It brought together several of my interests at the time: ghosts, folk traditions, the occult, history and Paganism (especially North European Heathenism.) That fascination has remained with me for over 40 years. What I present here is some accumulated material from that period with some personal comments and analysis. This book does not set out to be an academic book of reference. That task has already been accomplished by the excellent work of the Frenchman Claude Lecouteux, and I shall try to avoid duplicating too much of the same material as 'Phantom Armies of the Night.' Instead, I wish this to be an 'entry-level' book with an emphasis on the possible meanings and use of the material, particularly in a spiritual context.

In recent years we have seen the powerful Pagan imagery of the Green Man, the Sacred Hare and much more besides catching the general publics' imagination, outside of the narrow confines of folklore or religious history. Maybe the time has now come to embrace a darker side of the North European mythos, distorted, multi-faceted and enthralling: The Wild Hunt.

Chapter 1. What is the Wild Hunt?

In essence, the Wild Hunt is variously a train of spirits, usually mounted on horses but sometimes goats, pigs and other animals, plus witches, fairies, corpses, soldiers, knights and ghosts, riding as a hunt across the sky or land, and evident in a variety of forms across Northern Europe and Scandinavia. They are generally led by a known Pagan God or Goddess, or by a famous (or infamous) character associated with the land they cross. What beast or lost soul they are hunting for is also a variable, down to local legend and folklore. The hunt may be silent, but more often is described as having the awful din of shrieks, hunting horns, chains and thunder accompanying it.

The meaning of the phenomenon and the beliefs associated with it has been changed over the centuries. This is especially the case with the reinterpretation of it by Christian clerics, who seem to have seized upon it as a way of frightening their congregations away from sin, in the same way as they have adapted other earlier beliefs, sites and festivals.

What I, as both an established folklorist and modern Pagan find particularly interesting and impressive is the way that the tale has continued to fascinate, evolve and inspire storytellers, musicians, artists, dramatists, poets occultists and writers across at least ten centuries. It means many different things to a variety of people, in the same way as that other ancient mythological current, the Green Man has re-invented himself for successive generations and locations. I do not believe that there is a single definitively correct way of interpreting the Wild Hunt, and I think that the variations serve to illuminate the understanding rather than challenge it.

Of course, it is also known by a variety of names: as well as Wild Hunt it is also known as the Furious Host, Wild Army, Herlathing, Woden's Army, The Hounds of Annwn and many other titles you will find among the geographic chapters of this book. In this book, I will mainly try to focus on the material that fits the description above, since to be diverted by every isolated night visiting ghost or creature would require a much larger study. They will only be mentioned when they seem relevant or connected to the main themes. As usual with most scary things, it is mainly seen by night. There are stories of it from throughout the year, but the season of winters howling gales do most to suggest its' screaming pursuit across the skies, particularly between Yule and Twelfth Night.

In areas where ancestral spirits were believed to return to their former homes at particular periods including Yule or Hallowe'en (Celtic Samhain), food and drink may be left for the denizens of doom to placate or honour them, but elsewhere contact was shunned. There is the belief (still sometimes current) that the Wild Hunt or its' members are psychopomps, i.e. figures that herald the death of the viewer, either immediately or within the coming twelve months. Just as in other stories of visits to Other-worldly places such as the kingdoms of fairies, dwarves, elves and the Green King, care should be taken not to accept food, drink or any other gift, with the penalty being to be taken with them. Their appearance may also be credited with a warning of a significant calamity affecting a large number of people, such as fire, plague and war. In this way, one may start associating them with the Four Riders of the Apocalypse, yet the parallel is seldom drawn. They are Conquest / (alternatively Pestilence) on a white horse, War on a red, Famine on a black and Death on a pale horse, and their attributes are given in the Bible's Book of Revelations, Chapter 6. Maybe because they are often associated with the Christian Final Judgement Day, churchmen have avoided mixing them in with the earlier Heathen mythology.

A lesser-known aspect of the Wild Hunt is that at least two credible sources refer to a folk custom of a procession of masked people emulating the myth. This then poses the question of whether all reports of the procession are of a supernatural source? There is a possibility that some descriptions could be actual eye-witness reports of an ancient folk tradition, misunderstood by the viewers or later writers down of oral accounts.

Chapter 2. Wider geographic locations & variations.

As will be seen, most reports of the Wild Hunt and its' variants occur across Northern Europe and into Scandinavia. That is not to say there are not exceptions outside of that area or is it to say that all similar traditions have the same source. One can come up with a very similar story in different geographic locations without awareness of the other. Nor do I accept that because two things are similar, that they are the same. Consider a scarf and a tie. Both are made of fabric and wrap around the neck, but few people would insist that they are the same thing. In the field of folklore and mythology, one has to be very aware of not seeing connections without reasonable proof.

Let me give a brief (but not exhaustive) guide to the variants across several countries who do not feature in the Germanic, Norse or Celtic chapters. Many have dogs, ghosts and witches as members, but I have detailed more specific characters.

Czechoslovakia (and the older former countries in that area.) Called the Divoký hon or štvaní (wild hunt)

Greece Artemis is the Greek Goddess of the Hunt, so one may expect her to be associated with the Wild Hunt myth. She turns Acteon (who in popular legend had spied on her bathing) into a stag which is then killed by his own hounds. However, an Orphic Hymn (circa 3rd century) gives the female leader as Hecate, with a company of dogs and corpses.

Guernsey (Channel Isles) Here, the Wild Hunt is led by Herodias and has Sea Witches in its troop.

Italy It is strange in some ways to think that there seems to be no surviving evidence of belief in the Roman hunting goddess from being credited as a participant in Italy. In a work by Ovid, Diana sends a great boar to ravage the crops of the people of Calydon who had neglected her worship. The boar is eventually slain by a hunter called Meleager. However, there are other leaders to take her place: Theodoric the Great, Ostrogoth King of Italy and La Dona del Zoch (of Lombardy) as the Lady of the Game.

The Netherlands An unusual name for the myth here is Gait met de hunties/hondjes (Gait with his little dogs), but sometimes the name Derk or

Henske is substituted, and there is a 'glowing horse.'

Poland Here the Hunt is called: Dziki Gon (Wild Hunting with animals) or Dziki Łów (Wild Hunt)

Spain Estantiga (the old army), Hostia, Compaña, Santa Compaña (troop, company) and Güestia are some of the names given. From Catalonia comes a leader called Count Arnau (el Comte Arnau), a legendary nobleman from Ripollès, who for his reputation of cruelty and sexual misdemeanours is sentenced to ride to hounds (including Urco, the black dog) for eternity while his flesh is devoured by flames. His story is contained in a traditional Catalan folk song.

Switzerland Wuodan or Reinfrid von Braunschweig seem to be the alternate leaders of the Wuotis Heer (Wuoden's Army) or Dürstengejeg.

☐

Chapter 3. Germanic, Anglo Saxon & Norse connections.

Germany has several Wild Hunt tales, some of which are re-enacted as folk customs. The names of these hordes are variously Wotan's Hunt, Wotan's Army and the Wild Jagd. However, there are also traditions of females leading the hunt, including the Goddesses Perchta, Holda and a White Lady known as Frau Gauden. The latter is said to lead processions of dead children who were not baptised while living.

The procession is associated with fertility and is credited with bringing luck to planting, childbirth and the production of textiles. Some German legends include an old character called Honest Eckart, who rides a white horse and warns people to get out of the way. He has some similarities to the attributes of Odin: a broad-brimmed hat and long beard but was identified by Grimm as the Chamberer of Kriemhild from the Nibelungenlied.

In Austria & Bavaria the Wild Hunt leader Krampus, (an Old German term for 'claw') is a demonic horned creature who still survives. There is a custom in the area for young men to dress up as him. The tradition is also found in other Alpine regions, Hungary, Croatia and elsewhere. The figures wear horned masks and wear either black rags, sacking or goatskins. They drag chains, ring cowbells and clear the way with switches made of bundles of twigs. Sometimes their custom is merged with the Perchten.

Throughout the years, the mythology of the hunt adapted to suit the geographical area and the period. In the Middle Ages, for example, the lead huntsman included Charlemagne of France & Frederick Barbarossa.

A later German folktale states that the leader was Hans von Hackenberg, a semi-historical figure who died in either 1521 or 1581. It was said he had slain a boar and was then injured on the foot by the boar's tusk and died of poisoning.

As he died, he declared that he had no wish to enter heaven, but instead wanted to hunt. His wish was granted, and he was permitted, or perhaps cursed, to hunt in the night sky. Another version of the tale has it that he was condemned to lead the Wild Hunt as punishment for his sins.

But even behind this 16th-century character, lies a more ancient element, perhaps harking back to the original traditions surrounding the hunt. Hackenberg, it has been suggested, is simply a corruption of "Hakolberand" - the Old Saxon epithet for Woden, but also a mythical hunt leader in Westphalia.

Most of the names of leaders and hunts in the Germanic areas are Woden derived. Still, King Christian II is a popular leader in Norway & Germany while King Valdemar of Denmark (1157-1182) is associated with the hunt in Jutland. There is also a much-localised variant of Graf von Ebernburg of Zabelsdorf. I also came across Ritter Alke connected to a tradition in the Greifenhagen area.

BLACK SHUCK & OTHER HOUNDS.

Ghostly dogs are described in great detail in British lore and are known by many names. These black, spectral hounds bear almost as many names as the Hunt itself and are one of the most common features within the mythology just behind the named leaders. In the North, we find fierce Gabriel's Hounds. In Lancashire, they are described as monstrous dogs with human heads who foretell of coming death or misfortune. Some of the various groups of Hell Hounds of the Hunt bear a striking resemblance to the "Black Shuck," a solitary creature that has stalked East Anglia for centuries. In England, such lonely dogs are sometimes credited with being the ghosts of deceased people, changed as punishment, and will sometimes help people if treated kindly. Still, Black Shuck (known by a variety of names) is neither kind nor helpful: he is a psychopomp. i.e. an omen of death.

I have long been fascinated by the stories of Black Shuck & Wild Hunt in East Anglia. He is said to be a devil dog, black, shaggy-haired and enormous with fiery red eyes the size of saucers, and is most usually reported as appearing by himself, but has been associated as a member of the Wild Hunt. Maybe it is because of the canine connection with Odin/ Woden (Norse & Anglo-Saxon names for a similar Heathen deity). Still, his wolf companions were known as Freki & Geri (Greedyguts & Gobbler.) Woden also had two carrion birds, much associated with death and battlefields. Their names were Huggin & Munnin, which translate as Thought & Memory. He says that he would be upset to lose Freki, but it would be more terrible to lose Munnin. If you think about it, if you lose your memory, you do not even know yourself or kin or history, whilst thought would relate to new situations. According to the mythology, Huggin & Munnin circled the world each day to bring news back to their master, who was the chief god. Odin rode an eight-legged horse called Sleipnir and carried a spear named Gungnir, both handy in a hunt. In the Norse myths, he gets to choose the dead alongside the Goddess Freyja and the fearsome Valkyries, harpy like supernatural female spirits. All fit into the popular conception of them collectively being members of the Wild Hunt.

There are two famous stories of Black Shuck entering churches at St Mary's, Bungay, Norfolk and All Saints Blythburgh, Suffolk. You can see a burnt claw mark on the North door of the latter church accredited to him. The Bungay incident of 4/8/1577 was written up by Abraham Fleming in a black-letter pamphlet. Although it was August, there was said to be a thunderstorm overhead at the time. A man and a boy in the congregation were killed; as a psychopomp, there is a belief that looking directly into Black Shuck's saucer-like fiery eyes will cause death or disaster either instantly, or within a twelvemonth. At Blythburgh, part of the tower crashed down, and again two of the congregation were killed.

Sightings seem to never be more than a few miles inland from the East Coast, and range from mainly marshy, wet places, starting South in Maldon and around East Anglia, up as far North as York (Viking Jorvik), where he is known as the Barghuest. Other names include Galleytrot, Padfoot, Gyrtrash, Old Shug and others. There has been a theory that maybe he is the remnant of a fylga (fetch) sent to clear the coastal paths for raiding Vikings. Of course, it is speculation, but I find it at least possible - the locations all fall within the old Danelaw area.

The name Shuck is believed to be of Anglo-Saxon origin, from 1000 years before the Bungay & Blythburgh incidents. It is thought to derive from the Old English word scucca, meaning demon. The term is also used to describe Grendel and his mother in the Anglo-Saxon poem Beowulf. They are two monsters who dwell in marshland, have glowing eyes. Dr Sam Newton has pointed out that the East Anglian dialect word grindle, which is preserved in some Suffolk place names, means a drainage ditch or wet place, so this could be the origin of the name Grendel, as a creature who lives on the marsh. It also provides additional evidence for Dr Newton's theory which I support that Beowulf, although about a Swedish tribe the Geats, was written down in East Anglia.

Back in the 1970s, an elderly chap used to visit the Butley Oyster pub in Suffolk, where I used to go for singing sessions on Sunday nights. He arrived as white as a sheet one weekday night and said that he had been pushing his bike downhill, on the way to the pub, when he had encountered a sizeable spectral dog. Being generally afraid of dogs he had just kept going (and not stared in its eyes) but the beast went straight through him. Another old chap bought him a brandy to settle his nerves. This was commented upon afterwards as proof of how ill he looked - his benefactor had never been known ever to buy a drink for anyone else before!

Long after my original researches, I found an excellent book on the subject of the Black Shuck of the Wild Hunt. It even quotes me! Explore Phantom Black Dogs was the first effort to look at the psychology of the phenomena along with the folklore and can be recommended as a handy comparison to this work by a collection of authors.

St Guthlac, who lived as a hermit on an island in the fens at Crowland in the early 8th century, not far from Peterborough, was reportedly beset by spectral creatures attacking him, after upsetting them by singing Christian psalms. This is the same sort of reason that was blamed for Grendel attacking the hall in Beowulf, and yet more evidence linking the poem with an East Anglian origin.

Elsewhere the Peterborough area is mentioned again: in the Anglo-Saxon Chronicle (of 1127 AD) we find the following:

"...it was seen and heard by many men: many hunters riding. The hunters were black, and great and loathy, and their hounds all black, and wide-eyed and loathy, and they rode on black horses and black he-goats. This was seen in the very deer park in the town of Peterborough, and in all the woods from the same town to Stamford; and the monks heard the horn blowing that they blew that night. Truthful men who kept watch at night said that it seemed to them that there might be about twenty or thirty horn blowers. This was seen and heard.all through Lenten tide."

Monks at Peterborough commented upon it in 1132 and believed it was a response to the appointment of a bad abbot.

HERLA

The Germanic King Herla made a foolish deal with the King of Fairyland, and they each pledge to attend the wedding of the other's child. The Fairy King turns up to fulfil his half of the bargain, with a dazzling entourage. Then it is the mortals turn, but before leaving Fairyland, he is given a grimly stark warning and a small bloodhound as a parting gift: His trickster host says "Do not dismount until this dog leaps to the ground from the lap it is sitting in."

Later, a man in the procession dismounts his horse to check the harness, and to the horror of his friends turns to dust. They also find out from a traveller that centuries have gone by since they entered Fairyland, The bloodhound never leaves Herla's lap, so the whole party are destined to wander for eternity, becoming a Wild Hunt. Who knows why the Fairy King tricked them so – maybe they broke a taboo by eating and drinking in his land, against common folk belief.

Some say Shuck is a hound of the Herlathing, who can be heard howling on the wintry winds and seeking lost souls at the darker time of year. A 12th-century writer, Walter Map, describes the herlathing, which he related to this real person. However, some sources suggest that he is mistaking a nickname for Odin / Wotan for a leader called Herle. (Thing denotes a group of people in Old English.)

However, there is one other legend that Herla's Wild Hunt for some reason drowned in the River Wye, Herefordshire in the reign of Henry II and has not been seen in the area since then.

EDRIC THE WILD

An interesting tradition exists into the 19th century for a Wild Hunt led by Edric the Wild. He is mentioned in the Anglo-Saxon Chronicle, the Orderic Vitalis and a document by John of Worcester as a Saxon from Shropshire leading rebellion against the Norman occupation in the years immediately after 1066, with Welsh allies.

Legend says that he still lies within lead mines of a Shropshire hill, and is doomed to ride out until great Norman wrongs are righted. His appearance is said to presage war. Part of his legend is that he took a fairy wife, who made him promise that he did not reveal his past to anyone. When he broke the promise, he disappeared from the mundane world.

Edric is not the only historical character to reportedly lead the Hunt in England: Sir Francis Drake has the honour in the Dartmoor area. I wonder why that great Fenland Saxon hero Hereward the Wake, who also gave the Normans a hard time, did not end up attached to the legend, or even Robin Hood? Maybe they were, but the stories are lost, or perhaps they were seen as inherently 'too good' to deserve that fate.

FEMALE LEADERS

There are female leaders of the hunt in Germany: the Goddesses Perchta, Holda and Holle. They are sometimes said to gather up children, (termed Orla-gau) or give them presents. However, they also punish women who do not get their work done in a timely fashion, so woe-betide the lazy spinner! There exists a photograph of a folk tradition with costumed people called Perchten. They mostly have horns and fur suits but are accompanied by a figure resembling St. Nicklaus and his attendants. They can be seen in alpine regions of Austria and Slovenia, sometimes joined by Krampus.

SCANDINAVIA There are feminine leaders in Scandinavia to: Freyja or Frigga may lead it there. However, more often the Hunt is named after variants of the God Odin's name such as Odensjakt (Odin's Hunt) This Norse version of the Hunt was often seen chasing a solitary beautiful Otherworldly maiden. This maiden may be described as a 'wood wife' in Switzerland & Germany or even a mermaid in Jutland.

Denmark simply refers to her as an elf, but Sweden describes her as one of the 'hulder-folk.' However, I love the Danish legend of a hunt pursuing Slattenpat, an ugly old woman whose name translates as 'wobbly boob.' She throws her breasts over her shoulders to escape! King Vold is sometimes the leader of the hunt in Denmark, as is Valdemar Atterdag

Swedish folklore also describes the hunter 'Oden' as having red hair and beard, which are more associated with his brother Thor. Yet Oden (or Odin) can also be nicknamed Raudhgrani, meaning Redbeard, so maybe he shares his brother's hair colour. In Sweden, the Hunt is sometimes termed Hjaðningavíg, (eternal battle)

In **Norway,** the Oskerei is led by Sigurd Svein and Guro Rysserova, but Sigurdhr Fáfnisbani and Gudhrun Gjúkadottir from the Sagas put in an appearance. One named witch called Guro Rvsserova (Gudrun Horse-tail) can also make an appearance. She appears to be another name for Gudhrun Gjúkadottir, who had an unrequited love for Sigurd in the Sagas. There are also the Oskoreia and Asgardreia (Ride of Asgard, Odin's form of Heaven) and Gandreid (Ride of Death.) The theme of the Wild Hunt must have travelled with Scandinavian settlers (initially mostly from Norway) who colonised Iceland. The Yule Hunt seems to be the most popular name for it there.

Chapter 4. Celtic connections.

The Wild Hunt is not a purely Germanic / Norse phenomena. It has its parallels in the more Celtic areas as well. After all, until the sequence of Roman, Saxon, Norse and Norman invasions, most of Gt. Britain had a mainly Brythonic Briton population, which survived in some areas independently.

WEST COUNTRY The Gabriel Hounds are usually associated with the West Country, but I have heard references to them in tales from Yorkshire. In Somerset, they are called Gabriel Ratchets, and in Devon, they are also known as Yeth Hounds or Wisht Hounds. There is a strong tradition of them issuing from Wistmans Wood (one of the most magical places I know of) on Midsummers Night, led by Dewer (a politer name for the 'Old Gentleman' or Devil.) Some say that they chase the souls of unbaptized babies, while others argue that they are themselves such spirits, transformed by Dewer. The Elizabethan hero Sir Francis Drake is sometimes named as the leader of the Hunt in this area, particularly around Dartmoor and Buckland Abbey where he once lived. At the same time, in Worcestershire, they are known as the Seven Whistlers. Leicestershire also has a claim to the Seven Whistlers, and Westwood & Simpson established that they were associated with the calls of birds presaging death. In one example from Leicestershire colliers who had made a foolish bet were whisked into the sky and are destined to wander forever. A variety of bird species are credited with being their spirit forms, but the curlew seems to be a popular choice.

WALES *"And of all the hounds he had seen in the world, he had seen no dogs the colour of these. The colour that was on them was a brilliant shining white, and their ears red; and as the whiteness of their bodies shone, so the redness of their ears glisten. And he saw a horseman coming towards him upon a large light-grey steed, with a hunting horn round his neck, and clad in garments of grey."*

This is from the momentous Mabinogion story, at the part where Pwyll (Prince of Dyfed) dares to meet King Arawn of the Netherworld with his pack.

In Wales, the huntsman can also be Gwynn Ap Nudd, with the Cwn Annwn, better known as the Hounds of Annwn/ Hell. This is a bit of a misnomer as Annwn is a charming land of the dead compared to the descriptions of Hell. The ensemble seems sometimes to augment a separate Wild Hunt led by King Arthur and his retinue of knights who mainly seek a monstrous boar Twrch Trwyth. The role of King Arthur as a King in the supernatural realms was written about by Ettiene de Rouen in around 1168.

Then the wounded Arthur seeks after the herbs of his sister; them the sacred isle of Avalon contains. Here the immortal nymph Morgan receives her brother, attends, nourishes, restores, and renders him eternal. The lordship of the antipodean folk is given him. Endowed with faery powers, unarmed, he assumes the warrior's role and fears battles not at all. Thus, he rules the lower hemisphere, shines in arms, and the other half of the world is allotted to him. The antipodeans tremble at his faery sway; the lower world is subject to him. He speeds forth to the upper folk and sometimes returns to the lowest regions.

(Draco Normannius)

This theme was expanded in about 1211 by Gervase of Tilbury, who records that King Arthur becomes the Lord of the Wild Hunt and that keepers of royal forests reported that their experiences were of a hunt of knights and hounds claiming to be of Arthur's household.

There is one other Welsh Wild Hunt (which spills over into other areas). This is an evil priest Dando & his Dandy Dogs. He was said to have hunted on a Sunday, and when quarry could not be found cried that he would go as far as hell for a good hunt. A 'dark gentleman' appeared, as did some game, and so Dando has carried the pursuit on forever after with his black canine friends.

A traditional midwinter custom of Mari Lwyd (grey mare) in parts of Wales, now sadly decreasing, has the possibility of a link to the Wild Hunt. A scary horse figure (with an articulated snapping jaw) is paraded by a group of people who sing outside houses requesting permission to enter, eat & drink. They are rebuffed by other singers inside, singing alternating songs of insult to each other, before entry is allowed. The horse figure is similar to another one from the Hoodening Horse of Kent: the skull is on a pole, held by a person beneath an all-disguising and covering costume.

ENGLAND Cernunnos, the Celtic antlered lord of animals, merges with Herne the Hunter to provide us with one of the best known British Wild Hunt stories, centred on the Great Windsor Park and Forest. His fame has spread through the following text:

There is an old tale goes, that Herne the Hunter
(Sometimes a keeper here in Windsor forest)
Doth all the winter-time, at still midnight,
Walk round about an oak, with great ragg'd
horns,
And there he blasts the tree, and takes the
cattle,
And makes milch-kine yield blood, and shakes a
chain
In a most hideous and dreadful manner.
You have heard of such a spirit, and well you
know
The superstitious idle-headed eld
Receiv'd and did deliver to our age
This tale of Herne the Hunter for a truth.
    (Shakespeare, The Merry Wives of Windsor)

Michael Howard raises the question of whether
the traditional Abbotts Bromley Horn Dance is
connected to the Wild Hunt. I have had the
pleasure of observing this custom in
Staffordshire many times: 6 dancers with antlers
mounted on short posts perform a processional
dance around the village and its outlying farms
each September. The reindeer antlers have
been established as being more than 1000 years
old, (the animal became extinct in England) and
there is a written reference to the dance in 1686,
but another source alleges it was first started in
1226. Whatever the truth, the dancers appear as
two sets of three deer, clashing towards each
other, in the manner of rutting. The horns

comprise of two differently coloured sets of three pairs. Early September, when the dance is currently performed would seem an appropriate time for this. However, the early source states that it was also performed during the midwinter period. The dancers are accompanied by musicians, a man-woman, a hobby horse, fool and boy carrying a bow and arrow. It cannot be proved one way or another, but I would personally love to believe that it does have a connection to the Wild Hunt tradition, as do many of the Pagans who attend each year to witness it.

A hunt is also part of the proceedings in the traditional Antrobus Souling Play of Cheshire, a mummers play 'starring a wild horse.' It takes place around Hallowe'en, a time when both Pagans and Christians remember the dead. In some areas of Britain people used to go 'soul-caking': begging a unique cake that took away the sins or spirit of the recently deceased with it.

One cannot mention hunting legends in England without mentioning the death of King William II Rufus in the New Forest: A son of William 1st, he was very unpopular. Rufus refers to his ruddy complexion, not his blonde hair. He reportedly died from an arrow rebounding off a tree during a hunt. It seems pretty unlikely, even to chaps like me not into conspiracy theories. What arouses suspicions, even more, is that the huntsman who allegedly shot the arrow (Sir

Walter Tyrell) gets off scot-free! The huntsmen never even took his body away. It was left to a peasant named Purkis to find him and take him to Winchester Cathedral for burial.

One of the ideas associated with the death is that of the 'sacrificial king' who must die to save the land. Some people, in turn, link this to the theme of the Wild Hunt, but whilst entertaining and interesting, I feel that it stretches the facts too far. It is up to you as the reader to form your views but offer it here as an interesting aside.

IRELAND has the Wild Hunt of the Sidhe, or Lough Gur Hunt, led by Finn mac Cumhail and his hounds. Occasionally it is also termed the Fianna Manannan or Fairy Cavalcade.

SCOTLAND The Unseelie Court or the Hunt of Arthur O'Bower. (lead by a nursery rhyme character of that name) hold sway in Scotland:

Arthur O'Bower has broken his band
And he comes roaring up the land.
The King of Scots with all his power
Cannot stop Arthur of the Bower

If it seems familiar, it was used in the children's' book Squirrel Nutkin by Beatrix Potter in 1903 and has featured in many books of nursery rhymes. The poet William Wordsworth commented in 1823 that it was frequently recited at times of high winds when he was a child. His sister Dorothy sent it in 1804 to author Charles Laud in a letter. There is a theory that Arthur refers to the wind or even King Arthur, and it has been noted that one meaning for Bower is 'one that bends' – appropriate if that theory is correct.

FRANCE has it' s unique Mesnée d'Hellequin (Household of Harlequin) The character of the diamond-patterned costume, Harlequin spreads across many countries, and was an important character in the Italian plays that eventually developed into British Pantomime. In France, he was a character in Passion Plays that was an emissary of the Devil, but he is also seen as part of the clown tradition. He has even been claimed to be originated from Sufi spirituality. How that all fits into the general Wild Hunt genre is not easy to answer, but Vivre le difference!

Hole adds that the French also had King Herod hunting the Jews and the Maccabees of Biblical fame at Blois in what was termed Chasse Maccabei.

Chapter 5. Christian interpretations & influence.

As we saw in the last chapter, some characters end up as part of the hunt for their alleged sins, e.g. Dando. He is not alone in this: from the Christian Bible, we have the murderer Cain and Herod who committed genocide on Jewish male babies. Their names become attached to the

Wild Hunt in some areas. We also can detect a shift from the Hunt seeking game or a solitary female, to actively hunting for the souls of sinners or even un-baptised babies (of which the latter idea seems particularly loathsome from a God who is often portrayed a good and forgiving.) One could see it as the Christian church adapting an old Pagan idea as a bogeyman to frighten Christians into doing as they were told. After all, there is evidence in the form of letters that the church told missionaries to take over old Heathen temples and reconsecrate them, and to arrange Christian festivals to fall at the same dates as the ancient Pagan one, so why not extend that to folk beliefs?

Several Mediaeval texts detail members of the Wild Hunt being recognised by the living, who they tell that they are condemned to roam until their wrongs in life are righted. Lecoueux (2011) gives several detailed examples. Some imply that they will be able to leave the troop when this is accomplished, sometimes with the help of living people that they beg for help, prayers, or even to act as messengers. Some writers also refer to a very different phenomenon: ghost armies continuing to fight in the sky after a battle was long finished. Was this to warn of the horrors of war or to show that some warriors were so committed and involved that they continued to fight after their death? The question is open to conjecture. There is an additional theory forwarded by a bishop of Paris, William of Auvergne in the early 13th century. He reiterated an old belief that everyone's life span had already been allotted. If it was cut prematurely short by violence, the soul could not rise from the earth until the full period had passed.

There have also been supernatural sightings before a battle, such as the Angels of Mons in World War 1, but these do not seem directly related to the Wild Hunt. The Mons story appears to have been inspired by an earlier widely published fictional short story 'The Bowmen' by Arthur Machen, originally carried in the London Evening News of 29/9/1914, but much copied. The whole genre seems to be inspired by the notion that a nation fighting an 'evil' adversary will have 'God on their side', always debatable when both countries are nominally Christian!

People enjoy hearing frightening tales of supernatural beings, so by changing the emphasis of the Wild Hunt legends subtly, the church could fulfil a continuing a widespread need while advancing the new religion. Most people fear death, so to provide cautionary tales that persuaded them not to be sinful, and to demonise the old Gods (something that most incoming new religions attempt) there was much to gain. It was preferable to continue the folk beliefs of their followers, rather than trying to ban or suppress them.

That does, of course, give problems to anyone trying to discern the sources and meanings of the original Wild Hunt stories: one has to decide which data is of pre- Christian origin, and which may be later distortions or adaptations. Modern Pagans are generally quite adept and picking out such elements, but it is subject to human error. E.g. A tradition naming Woden as the leader may be seen as original and uncorrupted, but may still include later elements, such as what the prey is – a lost soul for torment or a spiritual quest for a feminine divine being? Or did the original story have lost souls as victims also? There seems no easy way to discern this other than by using 'gut feeling' rather than more scientific or academic methods.

One could argue that it doesn't matter; that it is what the story means personally to the individual in the here and now that is paramount, rather than try to investigate something beyond rational analysis. Happy the person of simplistic belief and faith, but it doesn't help those of us who are inquisitive, and equivalent to those ancient clerics contemplating how many angels would fit onto a pinhead. I have to confess that after many years thinking, discussing and analysing; I am no wiser than those who simply accept that the Wild Hunt just exists.

Chapter 6. Psychology of Psychopomps.

The concept of the Wild Hunt is frightening yet has remained popular over broad geographic areas and centuries. What is it that causes people to find a thrill from bogeymen, whether they be in film, book or story? From gruesome murders to monsters, car crashes and powerful predators, an interest in what should be repulsive seems hot-wired into the human psyche. What makes people be fascinated by stories often derided by others as superstitious or without factual basis, yet which survive for centuries within oral and written traditions? Some people say that they never feel more alive than when they are staring in the face of imminent danger (such as before a parachute jump, battle or motor race) and for those one can perceive an undeniable attraction. However, we are not all significant risk-takers.

There is a concept of 'safe fear.' i.e. being frightened of something temporarily, that one knows will be overcome and thus provide that post adrenaline rush sigh of relaxation when the monster is metaphorically vanquished, such as within traditional knight & dragon tales or a murder mystery. However, that does not seem to apply to the Wild Hunt, since most legends emphasise how it carries on for eternity, or at least for a very long time. So, could the pleasure derived from the story come from escaping the danger contained within it? The belief that by following the right actions and being more talented or better than other mortals, one escapes their horrible fate would seem to be an attraction. Indeed, the Wild Hunt myth usually contains advice on what not to do to be caught by it. That can, of course, be closely related to a spiritual concept, such as 'I have confessed my sins so will not be taken.' A large number of religions do have cautionary tales of what happens to followers who fail to follow religious rules, such as devils, disease, disasters, being turned to stone for dancing on a Sunday or going to hell. They often contradict the loving, kind and forgiving image of the god being followed. They could be interpreted as a way of controlling followers by fear rather than genuine desire to behave correctly. Frequently they are not contained within the central core of official teaching (such as the Bible, Torah or Quran) but persist as connected folklore.

From a Transactional Analysis viewpoint, who gains what in such an exchange? One could argue that religion increases control of the individual, while the individual perceives that they are getting useful advice from the faith to avoid danger. However, gain can be sought outside of a religious setting: a smuggler may spread a frightening tale to make sure that others avoid the area and time of night they are operating. The only possible return for the believer is that they may avoid (without necessarily knowing) the danger of what may happen to them if they witness the smuggling.

However, I believe that from a deeper psychoanalytic basis, there is a need for a person who is suppressed from doing whatever they want (theft, rape, murder etc.) to gain release via harmless fantasies: the need to be 'wild and free' transmuted into a vicarious thrill of safely exploring a dangerous 'other' world. (In Freudian terms, the Id which wants to act upon natural impulses freely is pleased by sensations provided by the ego, yet that is modified and controlled by the super-ego.)

Extending the psycho-analytic view to Jung, we can easily spot powerful 'archetype' models here: Jung theorised that universally, human brains are programmed to identify with a dozen different dominant metaphorical character types within its' collective unconsciousness. One could speculate that the psychopomps, death-bringing figures within the Wild Hunt are 'shadow' archetypes, i.e. qualities within the self that we most usually hide. We are all in our individual ways capable of bringing death, directly or indirectly. Still, most people do not expose that hidden side to themselves unless forced to do so by extreme circumstances such as war, being attacked etc. Therefore, to know about the archetype leader of the Wild Hunt is to have some more knowledge about one's inner self, and the potential personal ability to be responsible for the deaths of others. That may be illuminating, but also quite disturbing. Many people like to believe that they are morally 'good' and would not cause harm to others, even when attacked by them. However, in reality, they may react very differently 'in the moment'; as embedded self-preservation (or parental infant preservation) takes over at an almost unconscious level. If you believe that most women are naturally kind and nurturing, be aware that is likely to disappear if you try to take their child away from them (regardless of whether it is as a social worker or a paedophile.)

No wonder that the Wild Hunt seems to have spontaneously grown up within many different cultures and periods, without always necessarily being supported by incoming ideas from another geographic area. Of course, some folk traditions do travel and become adapted to each culture, but the popular ones appear to self-generate independently as well.

Turning the tables a bit, one questions the motivation of the characters within the Wild Hunt itself. Are they forever doomed to roam in pursuit of an impossibly large quest, against their wills, or are they there by their own choice for a never-ceasing joy of the hunt? I would suggest that examples of each are found within the stories. In essence, some are characterised as the souls of people who have misbehaved in life, who must seek pardon and forgiveness after a period of purgatory within this unique form of Christian Hell. Others are unlikely to seek Christian Heaven, since they are Heathen Gods such as Woden, competing to capture the souls of the dead or a completing a spiritual quest and delighting in it.

Consider even the semiotics of the phrase 'Wild Hunt.': Two punchy, monosyllabic words, with foreign equivalents, mainly following the same format. Wild is a much harder emphatic description than 'free' or 'natural' as choices, and much darker than 'exuberant' or even 'mad' yet could be supplanted by any of them and have roughly the same meaning. 'Frantic' would seem a reasonable substitute, except that it has two syllables. Similarly consider that 'Hunt': 'Chase', 'Search' or 'Pursuit' could have been alternatively used but are less visceral and more akin to a courtly pursuit. I think it no accident that 'Wild Hunt' is the definitive term that has survived, and in the modern vernacular 'does what it says on the tin.'

Chapter 7. Working with the concepts.

Do not allow the subject of this chapter to in any way persuade you to work with the myth of the Wild Hunt. As they say in the best of cautionary tales, "Do not try this at home." For a start, it represents the darker side of life and death, so for that reason alone is not for the faint-hearted, or those of doubtful mental, spiritual or physical strength.

You may argue that to do so will bring you nearer to the gods and goddesses of the old Pagan folk religions. As an experienced Pagan, I have to say that there are safer, more straightforward ways. Of course, many other religions would suggest that you should not get involved with anything that is 'supernatural' since it would inevitably lead you to evil and the Devil. I would point out that most major religions are based upon stories of supernatural happenings, miracles, auspicious prayers etc. yet they seem to mysteriously exempt themselves from this rule in an Orwellian 'Our magic good – their magic bad' sort of way. It also presumes that the individual believes in the concept of a Devil anyway.

OK, so you have decided to ignore dire warnings, good advice etc. and want to experience some contact with the Wild Hunt. Let us try and summarise some of the typical advice imparted via various stories and sources over the years that exclude staying away from it:

• Treat it with respect

• Do not get in its' way

• Do not accept food and drink while riding with it if you wish to return to the mundane world in common with other supernatural/fairy worlds.).

• Do accept other gifts but be aware that they may turn from gold overnight if you have been disrespectful. They could even turn into the corpse of your child.

• Lying flat on the ground, averting your gaze and holding on tight to any plants or bushes is a possible way of keeping safe in the presence of the Wild Hunt.

• Asking the hunt leader for a sprig of parsley to protect against madness or death.

• Offering to hold the hounds or wiping foam from the horse's mouth: either may turn to gold according to some German folk beliefs.

You could recite a charm to protect you such as this one, believed to be of 14th-century German origin:

Woden's host and all his men
Who are bearing wheels and willow twigs
Broken on the wheel and hanged.
You must go away from here.

(Gundarsson, trans. Höfler)

It was the translator of that verse Höfler that probably first proposed that the reason for a belief in the Wild Hunt stemmed from ancient cults or secret societies, with a quantity of academically structured arguments. Simek, the notable researcher on Northern European mythology, concurs, in stating that the widespread distribution of the Wild Hunt cannot be credited to a fear of the dead and winter storms alone. However, I would propose that if one wanted to experience a flavour of the Wild Hunt, it should be at the time of a winter gale, and with the memory of recently deceased relatives and acquaintances uppermost in mind. One may wish to call upon spiritual helpers, but it would seem inappropriate to call directly upon the fabled leaders themselves, but rather their intermediaries.

You may even try to be smarter than the hunt leader, (only those of a high IQ or supreme level of craftiness should try that with the master of mind games, Odin) but that would depend on how confident you are. There is, for example, a tale of a peasant outwitting Wod by winning a tug of war with him. He cheats by tying his end of the chain to a mighty tree. The wiser thing to do may be to leave a gift. There was a custom in Norway at the Winter Solstice to leave a sheaf or some grain in the field to feed the Hunt leader's horse. They also re-enacted the hunt with costumed dancers, who toured the locality punishing or rewarding behaviour of villagers. They may take the property of miscreants or give a blessing to those offering them food or drink.

These imitative processions are not unique to Norway. I.V. Zingerle wrote in 1857 about a similar situation in the Austrian Tyrol:

It was a kind of masked procession. The masked ones were called Perchten. They were divided into beautiful and ugly. The beautiful Perchten often distributed gifts. So went it loudly and joyfully, if the wild Perchte herself did not come among them. If this spirit mixed among them, the game was dangerous. One could recognize the presence of the wild Perchte when the Perchten raged all wild and furious and sprang over the well-stock. In this case, the Perchten ran swiftly away from each other in fear and tried to reach the nearest, best house. For as soon as one was under a roof, the Wild One could not have them any longer. Otherwise, she would tear apart anyone, who she could get possession of. Even today, one can see places where the Perchten torn apart by the wild Perchte lie buried.

(Sitten, BrSuuche, und Meinungen des Tiroler Volkes, in Höfler, p. 59)

Maybe those descriptions suggest a realistic way of learning about the Wild Hunt, by re-enacting it as a reconstructed revived folk ritual, although note the warning in the above passage. My personal experiences in related activities such as Mummers Plays, the Green Man and the Cutty Wren customs have been very positive in gaining an experiential knowledge that cannot be duplicated by academic study alone. I would recommend this as a realistic course of action to achieve an initial understanding that may progress to something more profound.

Chapter 8. Modern usage of mythology and imagery.

There have been several fictional books inspired by the Wild Hunt, many of which include it as the title or as part of their title or content. E.g. Authors Elizabeth Chadwick, Elspeth Cooper, Ashley Jeffrey, Graham Austin King, Lori Devoti and Margaret Randal to name but a few, with many more including it as a reference within a plot. Black Shuck frequently appears to, most recently in books by Piers Warren and Greta Jean. From the poetry of WB Yeats (The Hosting of the Sidhe) to a book by the Dark Materials author Phillip Pullman (Count Karlstein), the Wild Hunt is presented in a bewildering miscellany of forms.

As well as fantasy books, computer and complex role-playing games such as 'Witcher: Wild Hunt' there is also more than one film called Wild Hunt: a filmmaker named Will, 'Rev' Wright, made a short movie 'Wild Hunt' in Suffolk about a man on a quest to investigate the myths. I am featured in the film, which was premiered at Ipswich Film Theatre on Halloween, 2006. It should not be confused with the 2009 Canadian horror film, also called the Wild Hunt, which has Live Action Role Play (LARP) as part of its' plotline.

More recently, I took part in filming a documentary, which was shown on BBC4 in early summer, 2009: 'Beowulf & Anglo-Saxon Poetry' was presented by the prominent historian Michael Wood, and includes contributions by Dr Sam Newton and Brian Glover. It continues to be re-broadcast periodically. Dr Newton made the point that the scucca in Beowulf appears to be the same Old English language root as Shuck and that Grendel, the monster in the pool may have a connection to the East Anglian / Anglo Saxon derived dialect word grindle, for a wet, marshy place. I was pleased to relate the tale of Black Shuck in Blythburgh, where his burnt claw mark is allegedly on the church door!

There was also an East Anglian Border Morris side named after Black Shuck, who were brilliant, but now sadly disbanded. There is still a well-known Bedlam Morris side in existence with a big following in the Pagan community called Wild Hunt from Croydon who mask and draw upon the legends and imagery. The majority of UK Pagans are aware of Wild Hunt legends within Celtic and Germanic mythology.

The myth is represented in classical music to, with it appearing in works by Liszt (Wilde Jagd from Études Transcendentales).and Karl Maria von Weber's opera Der Freischütz. Rock music has many more examples than are worth listing, but check out the imagery used in song lyrics, album covers and names by bands such as Omnia, Therion, Watain, Furious Horde, Skyclad, Inkubus Sukkubus, Hounds of the Wild

Hunt, Falkerbach and Bathory. Also, check out the Swedish folk artist Tallest Man on Earth for a gentler approach.

You can also hear a song about Wild Hunt member Black Shuck on the Lowestoft rock band Darkness' debut album. Unfortunately, they were only able to find one word to rhyme with his name, and it wasn't luck! Great act, though.

I was recently surprised to find that the classic American rock song 'Riders of the Storm' was derived from the band Doors jamming around 'Ghost Riders in the Sky.' That is an American folklore survival of its European past telling the tale of Cowboy spirits pursuing the Devils herd of cattle. If you compare the tunes, you will find them very similar, but the late Jim Morrison, as much a poet and occultist as a rock singer, came up with some new lyrics. The Doors only got to play it live once, on the second date of their last tour, in New Orleans on 12th December 1970. The rest of the tour was cancelled when Jim left for France. His ex-partner Patricia Keneally-Morrison was a witch, who formerly lived in the town of Babylon USA between the Amityville house and Seax Wicca founder Ray Buckland. Jim died on 27/7/1971 (allegedly from a drug overdose) in France, maybe reinforcing the psychopomp idea once again.

Black Shuck is also known as the Black Dog, and that name crops up as the title of a Led

Zeppelin track with the lyrics "Eyes that shine burning red, Dreams of you all through my head." There is also a separate song of the same name by Humble Pie, and Black Dog is the name given by Winston Churchill to his bouts of depression.

More cheerfully, Black Dog is an excellent real ale brewery in Yorkshire, but with namesakes in New Zealand and New York) and a running club and race around Bungay in Norfolk.

Even the illustrious William Shakespeare uses the legend in The Merry Wives of Windsor, where Mistress Page wants to frighten Falstaff:

"Sometimes, if you sleep with an open window during the summer when the weather is fine and the nights are light, you might suddenly be woken up by a frightful hurly-burly out in the forest, right behind the house. There is shrieking and shouting, and the barking of a whole pack of dogs, the thud of horse hooves, the cracking of broken branches and so on. It's dreadful, and it's no time to be out in the forest for the hind hunt's on. You shake and quiver and your heart pounds at the sound of it. Sleeping's out of the question. If you're brave enough to take a peep out of the window in spite of it - O good gracious." even worse than hearing!

No doubt the legend of the Wild Hunt and its followers will continue to grow, mutate, fascinate, frighten and inspire.

In the beginning

Written for the Pagan Federation's Pagan Dawn magazine. Sorry, but I just couldn't resist placing the article with this title at the very end!

I was listening to an excellent talk by Dave Smith (Damh the Bard) at the COA Witchfest Midlands 2019 event, and something he said struck a chord with me; an idea that I had been thinking about for some time. He spoke about modern Pagans being the beginning of a new spiritual movement rather than purely the continuation of ancient Pagan beliefs.

It is essential, to know what has gone on both before and during the rise of the major world religions of today. Some of what we do is a revival of ancient beliefs and practices in a modern form suitable for this current age. To say that it is an unbroken historical path though strikes me as disingenuous: most modern experts acknowledge that Wicca, Druidry, Heathenry and general Paganism have only been known in their current form since the early 20th century. Early pioneers Gerald Gardner, Iolo Morganwg, Aleister Crowley, Alex Sanders, Osman Spare, George Pickingill and others have faced severe challenges to their claims of ancient authenticity in recent years.

That does not negate the valuable and ground-breaking work they undertook or the legacy that they have left to later generations. In most cases it is independently useful without the need for spurious claims of being part of paths going back to the dawn of time, unaffected by the persecution, interruption and influence of the Christian churches that controlled lives so effectively in the Medieval period.

Some modern writers and academics have made serious analysis and checked sources as diligently as they can to determine the roots of our current practices and beliefs; the well - respected Professor Ronald Hutton has been at the forefront of this, but Phillip Heselton, Doreen Valiente, Ray Buckland, Michael Howard, Isaac Bonewits and many others have done their best to sort the wheat from the chaff.

I know personally from my published analysis of Heathenism that this process is not always well received by people adhering to what may be life-long, firmly held beliefs. Humans, in general, tend to cling to the familiar and avoid change. We also have the problem that even when we have documents about ancient practices to follow, we cannot be sure that all the details and subtle nuances are there. When we have translations into modern English, current lifestyle makes us almost incapable of reproducing their intentions exactly in a completely different context. E.g. Does our modern 'political correctness' render us unable to relate directly to a time of very different social norms such as slavery, capital punishment, homophobia, limited life expectancy, racism and cursing?

While not wanting to compare Paganism with other religious paths, I do find it an interesting parallel that some Christian academics are revising their ideas about the very early church in the two or three centuries after the death of Jesus Christ. Some key insights have emerged:

1.   There were many disparate sub-groups with conflicting ideas, and some individuals isolated from all of them. The sub-groups sometimes accused the others of being 'heretical' in not following their version of the truth. Eventually, there was a severe rift between the Jewish originators and their Gentile converts.

2.   Written texts available now are often chance survivors of a much larger total literature. There is no guarantee that the best documents were the ones that randomly survived and lists of recommended books at the time frequently changed.

3.   Sometimes un-supported assumptions are made from quite small details, e.g. a picture over a catacomb tomb being used to tell us 'what was in followers heads' at the time.

4.   Influential leaders edited and suppressed texts they did not approve of and promoted those with which they agreed. They also condemned those who challenged them.

5.   The early church often had to meet in secret, risked death, punishment or at a minimum prejudice from local authorities. However, the first official significant persecution across the Roman Empire did not occur until the 3rd century, when the grassroots religion had expanded rapidly and become more organised. One source says that growth was about 40% per decade in the late 1st and early 2nd centuries. Because of that, they had to evolve a hierarchy and official positions and policies. Also, wider geography caused more diversity in their beliefs and practices.

6.   Despite the religion not being overtly political, followers found that they had to engage with specific political movements to enable them to follow their spiritual path or achieve their aims.

7.   Some of the imagery, stories and styles of worship were copied from other religious paths.

So, looking back at those points, how many of them echo the recent history of the UK Pagan movement? Despite a lack of a cohesive hierarchy, centralised authorised texts and a bewildering diversity of beliefs, practices and mythologies, we are regarded as a dynamic religious movement by others. Whether we agree or not they lump Druids, Witches, Shamen, Heathens etc. into one Pagan category in the same way as Baptists, Catholics,

Mormons etc. tend to all be classified as Christians.

If we agree that we will be regarded as the first generations of modern Paganism, what will be our legacy be to later generations looking back for clues about their origins? How would we like historians to categorise us? Should we be burying time capsules to be found by them?

I can only giggle at the thought of a Pagan committee trying to decide what should go in, and what not be included! Given that the more popular books, magazines, artworks and CDs selling the highest volumes are more likely to survive than the specialist works requiring more considerable study, our legacy may horrify us.

Maybe the archives and collections kept at places such as the Museum of Witchcraft and Magic at Boscastle or by the Doreen Valiente Foundation will become our future equivalent of the Dead Sea Scrolls! Sadly, some artefacts from some of the early pioneers were lost or sold overseas when they died. Stories about some of the major names in our movement have become confused or lost, as those first pioneers have died. We possibly need to individually ensure the future of our magical tools and documents by specifically planning where they go to in our wills.

In the late 1980s, when I 'came out' most Pagans kept their religious views secret and used pseudonyms and Post Office boxes for communication. There were the Satanic Ritual Abuse scares, and many esoteric shops were physically attacked. There were demonstrations and press campaigns against some Pagan events and activities. There were no moots and few conferences, and appropriate literature was hard to find.

While we do not live in a perfect situation, it is hard to make newer Pagans understand what it was like then. We now have conference and camping events in most areas, a positive relationship with a lot of the press, TV and radio, public moots and rituals and an important role within many interfaith communities. The media have confirmed what we long suspected: that despite a general policy of non-proselytization, we have organically grown in numbers to a remarkable degree. Confidence is such that the various Pagan paths have been well represented in the Census and the Police have a national Pagan Association. The Pagan Federation, which was once a very much small UK based umbrella organisation, has expanded to have a network of international branches across Europe and beyond.

We should be proud of what we have achieved in the last few decades: official recognition by HM Government as chaplains in prisons and hospitals, recognition by the Scottish Parliament of handfasting weddings, legal protection against religious discrimination at work or in the community etc. and recognition by other religions as a bone fide spiritual path. The UK Religious Education syllabus has been widened to include different religious paths. There is also an increase in trust between the various paths which has resulted in co-operative initiatives such as the Heathen & Pagan Symposium, Pagan Federation, Asatru UK, Children of Artemis, OBOD etc. While there is still much to do, these are all achievements made in a relatively short time, especially when compared to the struggles of other less recognised religious groups.

Like Dave Smith, I feel that this is an exciting time. We are into our second and third generations of Pagans originating from those who appeared in the mid-sixties, after the repeal of the Witchcraft Act in the 1950s and a culture that challenged old institutions and ideas. We have several advantages: the internet and independent publishing have enabled information to be exchanged at a rate never known before.

We are at least in theory protected by anti-discrimination laws and should not be afraid to invoke them. We can learn from the success or failure of other countries to establish religious freedoms. Public opinion on environmental issues has undoubtedly moved towards our long-held position. In contrast, some of the other older religious groups have drastically lost members and resources by not remaining relevant to modern views. However, this is not a time for complacency. We need to be individually and collectively active to ensure that the gains made are developed and preserved for the next generation and that we leave them a positive heritage and legacy.